Dedicated to the memory
of my mother,
Mary Husack Pavalko

Contents

Chapter 4
Recent Growth of the Gambling Industry   37

Chapter 5
Economic Impacts of the Gambling Industry   55

Chapter 8
Changing Perceptions of Gambling   95

Chapter 9
Compulsive Gambling   115

Preface

In deciding on a title for this book—*Risky Business: America's Fascination with Gambling*—my intent was not just to come up with something "catchy." Rather, the intention was to draw attention to the pervasive risks in gambling.

Risk and risk taking are at the heart of all gambling. In horse and dog races, the odds convey those risks. Bet on the long shot and you might win big; bet on the favorite and your winnings will be smaller. But, the risk of losing is greater on the long shot. High risk—high-potential return; low risk—low-potential return. The same principles that apply in the world of financial investing also apply in gambling. Buy a lottery ticket and the odds of winning are printed in very fine print on the back of the ticket. Virtually all casino games (poker is an exception because it involves a great deal of skill) have known odds and probabilities of winning and losing and "house advantages," and some bets are more risky and offer higher potential returns than others.

Risk is also involved when governments decide to legalize gambling. Whether they are starting a lottery, legalizing pari-mutuel wagering on horse or dog races, or legalizing casinos, governments and communities are taking risks. They are betting that their actions will create jobs and economic growth and that they will reap the benefits of increased tax revenues from the gambling businesses and increased economic activity. But there are risks involved—negative economic impacts and social costs. And to make things even more risky, legislative and public policy decisions are usually made without complete information on the risks and potential returns involved. The relevant information may not be available or there may be a need to make a decision quickly.

Finally, individuals are at risk. Gambling is a harmless recreational activity for most people. However, some people become compulsive or problem gamblers. Their addiction to gambling produces disastrous results for themselves and their families. Compulsive gambling is an addiction every bit as real as addiction to alcohol or other drugs. Deciding to gamble exposes people to this risk.

Every effort has been made to provide up-to-date information on the topics covered in this book. However, gambling is constantly changing and it is inevitable that discrepancies will occur. Some gambling venues will have closed and new ones will have opened. Proposals to expand or contract legal gambling will have been put forth, and some will have succeeded while others will have failed. Research will have raised new issues and reported new findings.

This book takes neither a pro- nor antigambling position. My goal is to provide an analysis of the nature of gambling and the role it plays in our economy and our personal lives. I hope that the information presented here will enable us to make more informed personal as well as public policy choices.

Organization of this Book

Chapter 1 presents an overview of the popular, scholarly, and therapeutic literatures on gambling. It highlights some of the main issues dealt with in the remainder of the book. It also identifies the kinds of gambling on which the book primarily focuses.

Chapter 2 looks at how mainstream sociology has regarded gambling. Largely ignored by sociological theory, gambling has been dealt with tangentially in research on crime and deviance, race and ethnicity, and social class. Ethnographic, participant observation studies are also summarized.

Chapter 3 deals with two major topics. First, we examine the history of gambling in the United States from colonial times through the 1960s. Next, we look at recent gambling developments in other parts of the world, with special attention to our closest neighbors, Canada and Mexico.

Chapter 4 focuses on the recent growth of gambling in the United States. The growth of major segments of the gambling industry from the late 1970s through the late 1990s is examined in terms of both the total amount of money wagered (handle) and revenues to gambling operators.

Chapter 5 deals with the economic impact of legal gambling on the United States. Positive and negative impacts at the national and local levels are examined.

In Chapter 6, the making of public policy regarding gambling is discussed. This chapter deals with how legislatures, courts, administrative agencies, and voters legalize or criminalize gambling. It also identifies factors that contribute to the success (or lack of success) of campaigns to legalize casinos. In addition, a case study of public policy making in Wisconsin is presented.

Chapter 7 deals with the transformation of gambling from a pariah industry to one of increased legitimacy and respectability. Contributions to gambling's increased legitimacy are discussed and include state action legalizing gambling, actions of the gambling industry, linkages between the gambling industry and other industries, and the mass media.

Chapter 8 summarizes research on two main topics: attitudes toward gambling and the kinds of gambling in which people participate. Attitudes toward gambling in general, as well as attitudes toward casino gambling, lotteries, racetrack betting, and bingo are dealt with. Research on social and demographic factors related to these different kinds of gambling also is reviewed. This chapter looks at the frequency with which people participate in different kinds of gambling, including casino gambling, lottery play, racetrack betting, and bingo. The social and demographic characteristics of lottery players are given special attention. The chapter concludes with a discussion of the extent of illegal gambling and the social characteristics of illegal gamblers.

Chapter 9 deals with compulsive gambling. It examines the way compulsive gambling has become medicalized and viewed as an illness. Basic characteristics or symptoms of compulsive gambling, addiction switching, and the relationship between compulsive gambling, mental health, and criminal behavior are discussed, as well as the instruments used to assess or diagnose compulsive gambling. The prevalence of compulsive gambling among adults in the United States and other societies is looked at, along with the prevalence of compulsive gambling among youth. The social costs of compulsive gambling, including the impact on individuals, families, financial institutions, employers, and criminal justice and human service systems, are also examined.

Chapter 10 deals with the treatment of compulsive gambling. Several treatment issues and models are discussed. The structure of Gamblers Anonymous and its role in the treatment process are described. Public policy regarding education, prevention, and the treatment of compulsive gambling is examined. The chapter concludes with a discussion of the role of the National Council on Problem Gambling and its affiliated state councils as advocates for the development of public policy on the treatment of compulsive gambling.

Chapter 11 looks at the future of the gambling industry. It focuses on technological developments that have the potential of expanding gambling in ways unimagined a decade ago. Virtual casinos, lotteries, and sports books are being developed and pose legal and regulatory issues that remain to be dealt with. The chapter concludes with a discussion of developments in in-flight and at-home gambling and some predictions about the future of the casino, lottery, and racing segments of the gambling industry.

Chapter 1

Introduction

During the past three decades legal gambling has become accessible throughout U.S. society. It has become a popular leisure time activity for millions of people. Lotteries are an important source of revenue for state governments, and the gambling industry is a major source of employment in areas such as Nevada and Atlantic City. The industry has also become an important economic force in communities in the Midwest that have riverboat casinos and for Native American tribes that run casinos and bingo parlors. The growth of legal gambling has also called attention to compulsive and problem gambling. For a small portion of the population, gambling is potentially addictive. Whatever economic benefits gambling may have, there are also social costs to consider. Clearly, there are a variety of issues and topics to be dealt with. The goal of this book is to shed some light on all of them.

How do we begin? An obvious first step is to examine what other people have had to say about gambling. There is a substantial body of literature on gambling. This chapter provides a brief overview of this literature to get the "lay of the land." Subsequent chapters examine these "literatures" and the issues they raise in greater depth and detail.

The Popular, Scholarly, and Therapeutic Literature

Although the literature on gambling is quite varied, it can be grouped into three broad types: popular, journalistic literature; scholarly, academic literature; and therapeutic literature dealing with problem gambling treatment. These three categories, however, overlap; for example, the numerous journalistic and scholarly accounts of treatment programs for compulsive gambling and the participants' experiences in them.

The Popular Literature

The popular literature on gambling covers a wide range of topics and includes an equally wide range of styles and approaches. An investigative reporting approach is often taken. Many times the literature focuses on individuals with criminal and underworld backgrounds who have been influential in establishing and developing Nevada's legal gambling industry (Turner, 1965). A related theme traces the connections between gambling (especially in Nevada) and organized crime. One book that epitomizes both these themes is *The Green Felt Jungle* (Reid and Demaris, 1963). It is highly moralistic and criticizes legalized gambling and Las Vegas in particular. This moral tone is present in much, but by no means all, of the popular literature on gambling.

The role of celebrities in the gambling industry has also received a fair amount of attention. This literature often has a tabloid quality and seeks to satisfy people's curiosity about the private lives of celebrities. Of particular interest is the role movie stars and owners of major motion picture companies play in the horse-racing segment of the gambling industry. Leo Rosten's (1941) classic study of Hollywood contains an especially rich description of motion picture celebrities as race horse owners and breeders and their role in the financing and founding of Southern California's major tracks: Santa Anita, Hollywood Park, and Del Mar.

The popular literature also deals with problem gamblers who have found their way to Gamblers Anonymous. Interviews with members describe how they started and eventually got hooked on gambling, their efforts to quit, and how gambling has affected their lives and their families' lives. Sometimes critical, sometimes sympathetic, these case studies provide valuable, anecdotal, but unsystematic portraits of compulsive gamblers (see, for example, Wagner, 1972; and Waller, 1974). In recent years, newspapers and popular news magazines have featured these types of reports.

A related literature focuses on the problem of compulsive gambling and warns of its dangers. Sometimes written from the perspective of a recovering compulsive gambler, it often slips into moralistic advice and crusades against gambling (for examples, see Estes, 1990; Geisler, 1990; and Moody, 1990).

The Scholarly Literature

The history of gambling in the United States, Canada, and Western Europe has been covered thoroughly (Ashton 1968; Campbell and Lowman, 1989; Elliott, 1973; Ezell, 1960; Findlay, 1986; Lears, 1995; Longstreet, 1977; Messick and Goldblatt, 1976; Tec, 1964). One may conclude from a reading of this literature that public sentiments toward gambling vary considerably between societies and change over time within societies. In the United States there have been substantial shifts in how gambling has been viewed. Widely accepted and tolerated during the colonial era and most of the nineteenth century, gambling was regarded as immoral, harmful, deviant behavior during most of the twentieth century. Since the 1960s, attitudes toward gambling have become more favorable as states have turned to lotteries, horse and dog racing, and casino gambling (for example, Atlantic City, Colorado mining towns, and the river towns of states bordering the Mississippi River) as sources of revenue.

A small but growing literature looks at gambling from an economic perspective. This literature addresses several different issues. One is how profits from legal and illegal gambling provide capital for investment in legitimate business enterprises (Turner, 1965). Another is state-sponsored gambling (especially lotteries) as a source of public revenue (Clotfelter and Cook, 1989). Gambling as a source of economic development is examined (Goodman, 1995) and a growing scholarly literature studies gambling's economic and social costs.

Psychoanalysts, psychiatrists, and psychologists have also been interested in the topic of gambling. Freud (1961) and other psychoanalysts have interpreted gambling in terms of the Oedipal complex and viewed heavy gambling as pathological behavior and evidence of an underlying neurosis.

Based on their clinical experience, psychiatrists and psychologists have contributed various theories about compulsive gambling and numerous case studies of problem gamblers. They have also tried to identify the personality characteristics of problem gamblers. Since the late 1970s, psychiatrists and psychologists have promoted the idea that problem gambling is an illness, that it should be viewed as compulsive, pathological behavior (Custer and Milt, 1985). This effort culminated in the inclusion of "pathological gambling" as a mental disorder in the third edition of the American Psychiatric Association's *Diagnostic and Statistical Manual* published in 1980. The most recent version of the manual (DSM-IV, published in 1994) includes pathological gambling as an "impulse control disorder."

Sociologists have approached the study of gambling using a variety of methods. Gambling has been looked at in relation to social class (Whyte, 1943; Downes, 1976; Zola, 1963) and race (Drake and Cayton, 1945; Frazier, 1957). Skolnick (1978) studied the control of legal gambling in Nevada by focusing on the political context of gambling and regulatory issues. There has also been a good deal of ethnographic research on race-track gamblers (Herman, 1967; Newman, 1972; Rosecrance, 1985; Scott, 1968), poker players, (Hayano, 1982; Martinez and La Franchi, 1969), and casino gamblers

(Oldman, 1974, 1978). Rosecrance (1985) has also provided an important analysis of the process by which problem gambling has become "medicalized."

Since the mid-1980s, the interest of sociologists in the topic of problem gambling has been increasing. Sociologists have also been involved in developing diagnostic instruments for identifying problem gamblers (Lesieur and Blume, 1987). Sociologists have applied survey research techniques to identify the prevalence of compulsive gambling in the general population and in special populations, such as youth and Native Americans. Political scientists have contributed a number of important analyses of gambling legalization as a public policy issue.

A primary source for research and writing on gambling is the *Journal of Gambling Studies*. Established in 1985, it was originally called the *Journal of Gambling Behavior* until the name was changed in 1990. It is jointly sponsored and published by the National Council on Problem Gambling and the Institute for the Study of Gambling and Commercial Gaming at the University of Nevada–Reno.

The Therapeutic Literature

Gamblers Anonymous has existed as a self-help program for problem gamblers since 1957. Psychiatrists and psychologists in private practice undoubtedly treated patients with gambling problems long before that. However, mental health professionals did not identify problem gambling as a serious disorder or develop treatment programs until the early 1970s. Consequently, treatment programs for problem gamblers have not existed long enough for a substantial body of literature dealing with what works and what doesn't to develop.

Nevertheless, there is a growing literature on the nature of compulsive gambling and its treatment. Treatment programs tend to be modeled after programs that deal with other, mainly drug and alcohol, addictions and the "group therapy" experience found in Alcoholics Anonymous groups. These programs (especially outpatient programs) often include regular participation in Gamblers Anonymous. These issues and programs will be discussed later in greater detail.

The Scope of Gambling

In its broadest sense, the term *gambling* includes a wide range of human behavior. Whenever we risk something for the possibility of gain, we are gambling. In this sense, gambling is commonplace in our economic life.

Buying, selling, and trading stocks, bonds, and commodity futures involve gambling. We put our money at risk with the hope that we have made a good decision and will be rewarded for the risk we have taken. In the world of investing, a basic principle is that the greater the return we stand to earn on our money, the greater the risk involved. It is not inappropriate to think of the New York Stock Exchange as the biggest casino in the world. (For a fascinating account of the concepts of risk and risk management in economic institutions and in the world of gambling, see Bernstein, 1996.) However, we will be dealing primarily with legal and, to a lesser degree, illegal gambling on a variety of games that we conventionally think of as gambling—lotteries, sporting events, horse and dog races, bingo, and casino table and machine games.

What This Book Is Not About

A few words of caution are in order. This is *not* a book about how to gamble, how to wager on specific games, or how to become a more skillful gambler. However, the world of gambling has a distinctive language, and the meanings of certain terms are not self-evident, especially to those unfamiliar with gambling. The main forms of gambling that are dealt with are:

- Betting on horse races, greyhound races, and the game of jai alai. This type of betting is often referred to as pari-mutuel wagering. Bettors bet against each other rather than against the "house," as occurs in casino games.
- Betting on sporting events, such as professional or collegiate football, baseball, and basketball games and boxing. Whether legal or illegal, organizations that accept wagers and make payoffs for these kinds of events are referred to as *sports books*. The term *bookie* refers to the person representing an organization that accepts illegal bets on sporting events and horse and dog races.
- Betting on legal and illegal lotteries. Illegal lotteries are often referred to as *the numbers* or *policy*.
- Betting on bingo, whether operated by charitable organizations or by casinos.
- Casino betting. This is the kind of gambling that can be found in the traditional venues of Nevada and Atlantic City, New Jersey, as well as in newer land-based casino locations (Native American reservations, Colorado mining towns, Deadwood, South Dakota) and on riverboats in Iowa, Illinois, Indiana, Missouri, Louisiana, and Mississippi. Casino games are of two types, mechanical games and

table games. *Mechanical games* include slot machines, video poker, blackjack, and horse races run on a video machine. *Table games* include craps (dice), blackjack, (21), baccarat, roulette, poker, and keno. Casinos (especially the larger ones) may also offer bingo games and sports books.

Gambling (especially its legalization and expansion) is an important political and public policy issue throughout the United States and in other parts of the world. Some people support it on economic grounds as a way of promoting economic development and tourism. Others oppose it on moral grounds or because they believe that it allows organized crime to become more involved in legitimate businesses and to corrupt public officials. Still others oppose it because of concerns about compulsive gambling and related "social costs."

Summary

This overview of different literatures on gambling has illustrated the variety of perspectives that have been taken on gambling. A popular journalistic literature has dealt with links between celebrities and gambling. It also has dealt with gambling in a moralistic way and warned of the perils of gambling addiction.

There also exists a scholarly literature dealing with the history of gambling, its economic impacts, and the increased social acceptance of gambling. Psychiatrists, psychologists, and sociologists have produced an extensive literature on the prevalence and social costs of gambling. Mental health professionals have developed a number of approaches to the treatment of compulsive gambling. All of these are explored more fully in subsequent chapters. This chapter also defines different kinds of gambling games and some related terms, but stresses the point that this book is not a manual for becoming a more skilled gambler.

Chapter 2

Sociological Perspectives on Gambling: An Overview

Gambling is a pervasive, extensive, and recurrent phenomenon in human societies, particularly in the United States. Consequently, it is surprising that gambling has not received more attention from sociologists. Sociological theorists have, for all practical purposes, ignored gambling. Thorstein Veblen, the early twentieth century American theorist, noted the existence of gambling but dismissed it as "an archaic trait, inherited from a more or less remote past, more or less incompatible with the requirements of the modern industrial process, and more or less of a hinderance to the fullest efficiency of the collective economic life of the present" (1953).

A coherent body of theory and research that could be called a "sociology of gambling" does not exist. At best there are scattered reports and analyses of gambling. This chapter attempts to pull this research and theorizing together and bring some order to it.

Gambling as Crime

Within sociology, gambling is frequently dealt with in the area of criminology. Here, the focus tends to be on illegal gambling and the role of organized crime syndicates in the operation of illegal betting activities. In this literature, gambling is typically viewed as a problem because of the profits it provides for organized crime and its potential for corrupting police and other public officials. Classical sociological theorists argue that illegal gambling per se is a "victimless crime," since those who engage in it do so willingly (Geis, 1972).

Gambling as Deviant Behavior

Sociologists working in the area of deviant behavior have also given limited attention to gambling. In an early and widely used text on deviant behavior by Clinard (1957) only 4 of the book's 577 pages were devoted to gambling, and the emphasis was on illegal gambling and how it might be curtailed. Although Clinard noted that people can and do lose all their money to gambling, problem or compulsive gambling was not viewed as an important topic of sociological investigation.

More recent treatments of deviant behavior have also paid scant attention to the topic of gambling. In the late 1980s, a popular text by Thio (1988) devoted a short paragraph to illegal gambling in a section dealing with organized crime. Similarly, Pfohl's (1994) history of the study of deviance notes that gambling has been considered a victimless crime. Goode's (1994) comprehensive treatment of deviant behavior makes no reference to gambling. Ward and his associates (1994) make reference to compulsive gambling in a discussion of mental disorders and the labeling process, but the topic is not treated as a major issue.

Public Policy Issues

Legal gambling has not been completely ignored by sociologists, however. Jerome H. Skolnick (1978) produced a landmark study of the control of casino gambling in Las Vegas. Based on fieldwork completed in the late 1970s, the study focused on state control of the casino gambling industry. While Skolnick touched on motivations for gambling and the impact of gambling on individuals, these were secondary concerns. At the time the study was completed in 1977, only thirteen states had established legal lotteries (Clotfelter and Cook, 1989). Since participation in gambling is likely to increase as its availability increases, the explosion in lottery and other forms of legal gambling in the 1980s and 1990s makes the public policy issue of the control and regulation of legal gambling even more relevant.

Ethnographic Research

A body of ethnographic research exists on racetrack gamblers (Herman, 1967; Newman, 1968; Rosecrance, 1985; Scott, 1968), poker players (Hayano, 1982; Martinez and La Franchi, 1969), and casino gamblers (Oldman, 1974, 1978). This research focuses on motivations for gambling, the subjective meaning of gambling, the life-styles of "professional" gamblers, and the social interactions of gamblers in "natural settings." The literature indicates that gambling is a way of compensating for work that is routine, boring, and frustrating. Gambling provides gamblers with an opportunity to exercise control, display their cleverness and skill, and have their accomplishments acknowledged in ways that do not occur in ordinary work activities. As Kaplan (1979) pointed out, people may turn to gambling in search of challenges that are not available in highly automated, routinized, industrial jobs.

This ethnographic literature also raises the issue of the ability of regular and heavy gamblers to control their gambling. Most of this research suggests that gamblers who get out of control periodically have the ability to "pull back," and gamble in controlled and limited ways. We will return to this issue in chapter 10, which discusses treatment for compulsive gambling and controlled gambling versus total abstinence.

Race and Ethnicity

There are numerous references to gambling in the sociological literature on African Americans. This research has not focused primarily on gambling, but includes gambling in its description and analyses of life in African-American communities.

A good example of this can be found in Drake and Cayton's (1945) study of Bronzeville, an African-American neighborhood in Chicago. Drake and Cayton focus on "policy" or the "numbers" game, an illegal lottery. Policy was a big business, betting establishments were numerous, and playing policy was a commonplace activity that was taken seriously. Policy games were a direct source of employment. Many individuals also benefited economically by providing goods and services to gamblers, such as fortune tellers and producers and sellers of dream books with lucky numbers and powders and oils to bring good luck. While this form of gambling was described as a widespread recreational activity involving men and women of all ages, there was no discussion of individuals becoming addicted to gambling or gambling compulsively.

A study of African Americans in Milwaukee suggests that policy games were a commonplace activity around the time of World War II. In the early 1940s, there were campaigns to curb policy games (and bingo, raffles, and illegal horse betting) in African-American neighborhoods, but not in other parts of the city (Trotter, 1985, 202).

While Drake and Cayton dealt with working-class and poor African Americans, Frazier's (1957) analysis of middle-class African Americans at midcentury commented on the pervasiveness of gambling. One of Frazier's main conclusions was that successful middle-class African Americans had created and lived within a social world of delusions and make-believe, and that gambling was one of many mechanisms for escaping from frustrations, the acknowledgment of their lower status, and lack of acceptance in the larger society. Although betting on horses and playing the numbers (policy) were common among this "black bourgeoisie," poker was identified as the most popular form of gambling. Frazier noted that "gambling, especially poker, which has become an obsession . . . offers the chief escape into delusion. Among the black bourgeoisie it is not simply a device for winning money. It appears to be a magical device for enhancing their self-esteem through overcoming fate" (Frazier, 1957: 190). Frazier's discussion of gambling, and especially poker playing, indicated that gambling was common among both men and women.

Because Frazier's interest was in the function of gambling for middle-class African Americans, he did not deal directly with the issue of addictive or compulsive gambling. However, there are hints that, for some people, gambling had gotten out of control. For example, he noted that "children often say that they had a happy family life until 'mama took to poker'" and that for many people poker "has an irresistible attraction which they often confess they cannot overcome" (Frazier, 1957: 190, 191). Thus, while Frazier present a tantalizing glimpse of what might be called compulsive gambling, the idea was not fully explored and developed.

The literature on Japanese Americans also contains some important comments on gambling among members of this ethnic group. Harry H. L. Kitano (1976), an authority on criminal and deviant behavior among Japanese Americans, noted that between 1940 and 1970 drunkenness and gambling were the main offenses for which Japanese Americans were arrested. Although African Americans and Americans of European ancestry also had high arrest rates for drunkenness, they were much less likely to be arrested for gambling. Kitano suggested that gambling is a "culturally based trait." Gambling is widespread in Japan, and Kitano noted that it was the "number one offense" in Japan from 1907 to 1931. He also indicated that Nevada gambling junkets originating in Los Angeles and San Francisco drew heavily on the Japanese-American populations of those cities (Kitano, 1976: 146).

Analyses of the history of Chinese Americans also make reference to gambling. Gambling appears to have been widespread among Chinese men who came to California and other areas of the West in the late nineteenth century to work as laborers on railroads, in mining, and in agriculture. For men living in relative isolation, and without families, gambling was an important form of recreation and entertainment. Lyman (1974) pointed out that early Chinese immigrants to the United States came as "sojourners" intending to make money and return to their families in China as soon as possible. The low-skill, low-status, and low-paying jobs they found made this dream difficult to realize. Gambling offered the possibility and hope of quick and dramatic wealth, in effect, a short-circuiting of the slow process of accumulation of wealth through hard physical labor. One observer of San Francisco's Chinatown in the 1930s noted that gambling persisted among transient Chinese men "because it is the only social outlet that holds out the possibility of economic freedom" (Leong, 1936: 192). According to Lyman, gambling in the Chinatowns of San Francisco, New York, Chicago, and Vancouver was part of the routine of daily life well into the 1960s, especially for older, single men.

Social Class

The topic of gambling has received some attention in the enormous body of sociological literature on social class. However, the relationship between gambling and social class has not been the primary focus of this research. Rather, gambling has been dealt with incidentally in the description and analysis of life at different social-class levels.

Whyte's (1943) classic study of working-class youth in a section of Boston in the late 1930s made numerous references to gambling. Gambling was a commonplace activity among the "corner boys" he studied. While playing the numbers and betting on horses and prize fights were easy to do given the presence of illegal bookmakers and numbers runners in the community, betting extended to a wide range of individual and team competitions organized by the boys themselves. Whyte's analysis gives the impression that gambling was part of the fabric of everyday life.

Another important study of class and gambling is Zola's (1963) analysis of the functions of gambling among working-class men in an unidentified "large New England city." The locale for the study was a neighborhood bar and grill frequented mainly by men who lived in the immediate area. They were mainly of Italian and Polish ancestry; the vast majority were over the age of thirty and were regularly employed. The bar was a place where they spent much of their leisure time. They stopped in after work, spent days off and vacation days there, and many who worked nearby or drove trucks or taxis stopped in frequently during the workday. Gambling was the main focus of interaction in the bar. It consisted mainly of betting on horse races, with some betting on baseball games. Wagers were made through a bookmaker, who was a regular fixture in the bar.

The patrons of the bar Zola studied were a close-knit group, and participation in betting contributed to group cohesion. The accumulation of winnings per se was not the objective of the wagering. Rather, wagering was a means of "beating the system," and those who managed to win were the objects of admiration, attention, and praise from other members of the group. Gambling, especially if one was successful at winning, also served as a way of overcoming the sense of futility that pervaded the lives of these working-class men. To beat the system, to rationally choose the winning horse or team, or to beat the odds gave these men a sense of control over their fates, if only momentarily. In this sense, gambling provided the possibility of achieving something—control, evidence of success, admiration, a sense of accomplishment, and recognition for it—that was not readily available in their lives and especially in their work. Gambling offered the chance of being "somebody" rather than "nobody."

In the early 1970s, a study of gambling behavior in Great Britain found that extremely poor people were the least likely to gamble, but that very poor women gambled more often than very poor men. In general, frequency of gambling increased as income increased. In terms of social class, middle-class people (those in white-collar occupations) gambled less frequently than working-class people (those in blue-collar occupations) (Downes, 1976).

This British study also tested Devereux's (1949) hypothesis that gambling serves as a "safety valve" function. Given the contradiction between the Protestant ethic and the inequalities of modern capitalism, gambling should be less frequent among middle-class Protestants than among middle-class non-Protestants or working-class Protestants. The study found inconsistent results due in part to the small number of non-Protestants in the sample. However, after weighting procedures were used, middle-class Anglicans were found to be more involved in gambling than middle-class Catholics (contrary to the theory), and working-class Catholics were slightly more involved in gambling than working-class Protestants (which was consistent with the theory).

Downes also tested Herman's (1967) theory that the decision-making involved in gambling (especially handicapping horse and dog races) appeals to those who lack opportunities to make decisions in their work. When people with different levels of job autonomy were compared, there was no difference in their belief that skill is involved in gambling. (The claim that skill is involved was almost universal, that is, there was very little variation on this variable.)

Downes investigated Goffman's (1961, 1967) idea that gambling involves risk-taking for which there are few opportunities in ordinary work activities given the bureaucratization and routinization of modern life. The findings of the study were mixed. Downes found no relationship between social class and (self-described) risk taking, although the more routinized jobs of working-class people might be expected to lead to more risk taking in their nonwork lives. No relationship between risk taking and frequency of gambling was found either. However, among working-class people, risk takers were found to be more likely to be gamblers, and among middle-class people, risk takers were less likely to be gamblers.

Chapter 8 looks at recent research in the United States on how such indicators of social class position as educational attainment and income are related to peoples' attitudes toward gambling and the kinds of gambling in which they participate.

Summary

A review of how sociologists have viewed gambling indicates that it has not been a central focus of sociological theory and research. Sociologists studying crime have dealt mainly with illegal gambling, and their interest has been minimal. Studies of deviant behavior have paid little attention to the topic of gambling.

The study of the regulation and control of casino gambling and of gamblers in their natural settings both have been done from a sociological perspective. The role of gambling in the lives of members of certain racial and/or ethnic groups (African Americans, Japanese Americans, and Chinese Americans) has received some attention, but only as an interesting sidebar in analyses of ethnic communities and groups.

Research on social class and gambling suggests that gambling is a commonplace and widespread activity in working-class communities. While it may serve different functions or purposes for different class levels, gambling appears to enhance the status of working-class people in low-status occupations.

Chapter 3

Gambling in the United States and in Other Societies

The recent explosion of legal gambling in the United States has many parallels and continuities with the past. To appreciate the significance of gambling in contemporary American society, it helps to have an historical perspective.

Although the main focus of this book is gambling in the United States, it is also useful to examine recent gambling developments in other societies. Both similarities and differences occur in the kind and amount of gambling that exists in other societies. For millions of Americans living in close proximity to Canada, developments in that country have provided easy access to casino gambling. Mexico and the Caribbean islands are popular vacation destinations for U.S. citizens. The availability of gambling in these areas affects gambling opportunities too. This chapter provides a general overview of the most important developments and issues in other parts of the world.

I. Nelson Rose (1986), a lawyer who specializes in the study of legal aspects of gambling, has argued that gambling has gone through three historical phases in the United States. During the colonial and post-revolutionary period of our history, gambling thrived. Governments supported and encouraged gambling, primarily in the form of lotteries. The first phase ended with the ascendancy of Jacksonian morality and a number of scandals involving outright fraud in the conduct of lotteries. By 1862, every state except Missouri and Kentucky had outlawed lotteries (Sullivan, 1972: 50–51). The second phase began after the Civil War. Many southern states, desperate for revenues, turned to lotteries, and jurisdictions legalized gambling houses in order to tax them. With the westward movement of the frontier, gambling became pervasive, and legal prohibitions were difficult to enforce. In the 1890s, scandals surrounding Louisiana's lottery resulted in the passage of federal antilottery legislation. Many states also passed legislation banning

15

lotteries, often writing the ban into state constitutions. Along with the demise of lotteries, betting on horse races became tainted and by 1910 there was virtually no legal gambling in the United States save for a few horse race tracks (Dombrink and Thompson, 1990: 11; Weinstein and Deitch, 1974: 13–14). According to Rose (1986, 1995) the third phase began during the Great Depression of the 1930s. Nevada re-legalized gambling in 1931, and during the decade of the 1930s, twenty-one states opened racetracks with pari-mutuel betting. The illegal lottery run by organized criminal syndicates and known as "the numbers" or "policy" became very popular, particularly in urban areas. In 1964, New Hampshire began the first legal lottery of the century, setting off a growth in legal gambling that continues up to the present (Rose, 1986, 1995).

Gambling in America

Colonial America

Gambling has been part of American culture since the original colonies were founded. Between 1612 and 1615, the Virginia Company conducted four lotteries in England to raise money for its foundering colony in North America. Lotteries had been used in England since the mid-1500s to raise money for public works projects, so the use of a private lottery was a familiar strategy. In the Virginia colony itself, company officials attributed their lack of success to the "idleness and other vices" (including particularly gambling) of the colonists (Findlay, 1986).

Ambivalence about gambling was apparent early during the colonial period. Gambling was a widespread and popular recreational activity in England during most of the 1600s, and many colonists brought with them pro-gambling sentiments. Horse racing, cockfighting, card games, dice, and lotteries were the main forms of gambling that thrived in the colonies. However, Puritans and Quakers had very different views on gambling.

For Puritans, gambling was a double vice: it was unproductive idleness and a profaning of God. Gambling and leisure activities were seen by the Puritans as a waste of time that could, and should, be spent on productive work. The very act of gambling was also seen as blasphemy since it implied asking God for help in bringing about a favorable (winning) outcome in a game. Such appeals to providence were seen as frivolous and the equivalent of taking God's name in vain, since they represented an appeal for divine intervention in trivial and sinful matters. Consequently, the leaders of the Massachusetts Bay Colony passed a variety of (largely ineffective) laws against gambling and other leisure activities and pastimes that were regarded as a waste of time (Sasuly, 1982).

In Pennsylvania, Quakers shared a similar aversion to idleness and were committed to establishing a colony based on religious principles. Laws passed between 1682 and 1740 attempted to ban all forms of gambling and were fairly successful as long as the colony was religiously homogenous. But as time went on and the colony became more diverse in terms of religion and ethnicity, gambling became more common. The colony's ban on lotteries also created friction with the English Crown since English lottery tickets could not be sold in the colony (Findlay, 1986: 21).

In other colonies—Virginia, Maryland, New York, and South Carolina—the progambling perspective common in England came to predominate. Virginia landowners attempted to emulate the English aristocracy by developing horse racing into a major leisure activity. The breeding and racing of horses was seen as a "gentlemen's sport," a cultural prerogative that set the upper class apart from the common people. This class dimension to racing can be seen in a case that came to court in York County in 1674. A planter had raced his horse against that of a tailor. The tailor was punished with a fine, and the planter was put in the stocks for one hour. The grounds for this was that it was "contrary to Law for a Laborer to make a race, being a sport only for Gentlemen" (Findlay, 1986: 23). In New York, Maryland, and South Carolina horse racing was a popular pastime. In South Carolina and other southern frontier regions, cockfighting was also popular.

In Colonial America both public and private lotteries were commonplace. Lotteries were usually operated for a specific purpose or project (rather than for ongoing activities as is the case with contemporary lotteries). Once money was raised for a project, the lottery would cease operation, and another one might start up for another purpose. Lotteries were also used to raise money to start what would become the nation's most prestigious private Ivy League universities. Private lotteries were used to sell property, such as land and homes, that was too expensive for single individuals to purchase. These private lotteries, really a special type of commercial transaction, were the first lotteries to become popular and, because of the potential for fraud, the first to become regulated (Ezell, 1960).

Colonial governments also used lotteries to raise money. They were, in effect, an alternative to unpopular taxation. Initially, private sponsors were chartered to run the lotteries, but charges of fraud led to government regulation in most colonies. Lotteries of this kind were used to support churches, charities, hospitals, and schools, as well as to build bridges, roads, wharves, and defense installations.

After the beginning of the Revolutionary War, the Continental Congress authorized a lottery to raise $1.5 million dollars to finance the conflict with Britain. People were urged to buy tickets as a way of contributing to "the great and glorious American Cause" (Ezell, 1960). Participation in the lottery was virtually equated with patriotism, but it was largely unsuccessful. There were no prizes. Instead, ticket buyers were issued promissory notes. If England had won the war, the tickets would have been worthless. This example illustrates governmental ambivalence toward gambling. Prior to the Revolutionary War, the Continental Congress had condemned gambling. In an effort to develop "revolutionary virtue," the Congress admonished people to give up "every species of extravagance and dissipation, especially all horse-racing, and all kinds of gaming, cock-fighting . . . and other expensive diversions and entertainments" (cited in Fabian, 1990: 25).

Despite the pervasiveness of gambling in colonial America, it was seen as a vice in many quarters, especially by religious leaders. Fabian (1990) has provided a detailed account of religious opposition to gambling. Throughout the colonies, gambling was criticized as a habit-forming, all-consuming passion that led to idleness, financial irresponsibility, dishonesty, and a passion for material gain. From a religious perspective, gambling turned people away from God; when they lost, they blasphemed the Almighty, and when they won, they attributed it to their own skill or cleverness. In Virginia in the 1750s, Samuel Davis, an evangelical Presbyterian minister, even blamed droughts and military defeats on Virginians' passion for gambling (Fabian, 1990: 24).

The Nineteenth Century

Many lotteries openly violated their charters by extending the time periods for ticket sales (thereby increasing their profits), overselling tickets, and rigging the outcome. Scandals involving the bribery of public officials by lottery operators were commonplace. In some cases, lottery operators simply disappeared after selling their tickets. Early in the nineteenth century, reformers and charities attributed pauperism (impoverishment) to lotteries as well as excessive alcohol consumption (Ezell, 1960).

In the 1820s, an antilottery movement was spearheaded by the Society of Friends (Quakers), which played an important role in the disappearance of lotteries from most northern states by the 1840s. Public disillusionment with lotteries became evident in the south as well. By 1860, only three of the thirty-three states permitted lotteries (Weinstein and Deitch, 1974). However, with the outbreak of the Civil War, many southern states turned to lotteries as a source of revenue for military expenditures. In 1868, Louisiana established a lottery that lasted for twenty-five years amid recurring scandals. Antilottery sentiment developed again in the waning decades of the nineteenth century, fueled to a significant degree by the scandals surrounding the Louisiana lottery. By 1900, thirty-six of the forty-five states had outright prohibitions against lotteries and, in some cases, other forms of gambling (Joyce, 1979).

After the Revolutionary War, gambling moved westward with the frontier. In the 1800s, new forms of gambling and new types of gamblers appeared in the lower Mississippi Valley from St. Louis to New Orleans. In river towns such as Vicksburg, Natchez, Memphis, and New Orleans, casino games—faro, craps, monte, poker, and roulette—became popular. The spread of gambling was not without its opponents, however. In 1835, outraged citizens of Vicksburg hanged five faro dealers perceived as promoting immorality (Fabian, 1990). Although the Mississippi riverboat gambler remains a popular image of this era, land-based public gambling establishments actually preceded the riverboat.

Gambling thrived in the gold-mining areas of California and silver-mining areas of Nevada in the 1840s and 1850s. As Dombrink and Thompson (1990) have pointed out, "The combination saloon/bordello/ gambling hall became the main center for recreation for the thousands of miners and cowboys, who were mostly on their own, without families or wives" (p. 10).

During the 1850s, gambling also thrived in the frontier towns of Kansas City and Denver, as well as in San Francisco, where it was a major part of the fabric of social life. Following the discovery of gold and the ensuing "gold rush," commercial gambling establishments emerged throughout California. Gambling was viewed like any other business. Although commonplace throughout California, nowhere did gambling flourish as in San Francisco. Plush multistory clubs, as well as makeshift tents, were erected as gambling centers. Gambling was an important source of municipal revenue, and the city licensed, regulated, and taxed these businesses.

Commercial gambling also developed in eastern and midwestern cities. Illegal numbers and policy games drew customers from the urban working class and legal gambling houses served mainly the politically powerful upper class. Off-track bookmaking syndicates also emerged by the 1890s (Haller, 1979; Sasuly, 1982). Technically operating outside the law, protection from police and political interference was essential for their success and survival. Consequently, gambling entrepreneurs created elaborate relationships with the police and political organizations. According to Johnson (1977), they "created complex and subtle connections among themselves, their customers, politicians and the police which redefined the context in which law enforcement occurred" (p. 18).

Many believe that organized crime syndicates emerged in the 1920s in response to the demand for alcohol during the decade of Prohibition. However, they made their appearance much earlier. Haller (1979) pointed out that between 1880 and 1905,

Gamblers and vice entrepreneurs generally exercised an influence on local politics and law enforcement that has seldom been equalled since that time. In many neighborhoods, it was not so much that gambling syndicates influenced local political organization; rather, gambling syndicates were local political organizations. . . . Long before national prohibition and the development of bootlegging, then, there had already been close ties among gambling syndicates, vice activities, politics, sports, and entertainment. (P. 88)

The First Half of the Twentieth Century

During the first half of the twentieth century, legal gambling was relatively rare in the United States. This section highlights some of gambling's more important developments to illustrate both government action and public interest in gambling. Two key developments—the reemergence of lotteries and the growth of the casino segment of the gambling industry are noted, but will be discussed more fully in chapter 4.

Between 1894 and 1964, there were no government-operated or government-licensed lotteries in the United States. During the Great Depression of the 1930s, lottery proposals were introduced in the legislatures of five northeastern states. The profits were to be used for general relief and unemployment compensation, but none of these proposals succeeded.

The Irish Sweepstakes was started in 1930 and remained popular until World War II, when its operation was suspended. In 1938, a national survey found that 13 percent of the population had purchased a Sweepstakes ticket. Following the war, its popularity grew once again.

During the first several decades of the twentieth century, many religious and charitable organizations throughout the country held illegal bingo games and raffles. The first state to legalize bingo was Rhode Island (1937), followed by New Hampshire (1949) and New York (1954). By 1973, thirty-four states had legalized charity bingo, which was seen as a harmless alternative to illegal betting on numbers and policy games.

A popular form of gambling during the colonial era and the first half of the nineteenth century, horse racing was adversely affected by the antigambling, antilottery sentiment of the late nineteenth century as well as by religious crusaders and opportunistic politicians running on "reform" platforms. In 1900 only three states (Maryland, Kentucky, and New York) permitted pari-mutuel betting. But by 1911, six states allowed betting at racetracks, and in 1930, the number was up to twenty-one. During the Depression decade of the 1930s, states turned to racing as a source of revenues. By 1938, another eleven states had legalized (and were taxing) pari-mutuel betting (Rosecrance, 1988).

Except for the period of 1910 to 1930, casino gambling has been legal in Nevada since 1869. From 1931 to 1945, the licensing and control of casinos was a local (county) responsibility. There is no doubt that a large amount of criminal syndicate money from the East flowed to Nevada and funded the early "modern" casinos. In 1945 the state of Nevada took over licensing and tax collecting responsibilities. The industry, however, was not regulated until after 1955 when the state established a separate gaming control agency.

Besides Nevada, the only other state to legalize casino gambling, albeit briefly, was Florida. In addition to legalizing pari-mutuel betting, the state legalized slot machines in the 1930s as a source of revenue. The experiment with slot machines ended in 1937 after religious organizations complained that those least able to afford it (poor and working-class people) were squandering their money on the machines. While slot machines (which numbered 12,500 at one point) were destroyed with great ceremony, they continued to operate with little attention from law enforcement officials in private clubs catering to the wealthy (Rosecrance, 1988).

A variety of illegal gambling activities both flourished and were the targets of police crackdowns during the first half of the twentieth century. With the disappearance of legal lotteries in the early 1900s, illegal lotteries—policy or numbers—flourished, and their popularity has continued to this day.

Throughout the United States, illegal casinos became the target of political reformers and religious zealots. In many cases, casinos were closed down with a great deal of fanfare and media attention, only to reopen after public attention was distracted by other events (Rosecrance, 1988).

The 1950s to the 1970s

Since the late 1950s, Nevada (especially Las Vegas and Reno) has become a popular gambling destination resort. This is due to several factors. First, the industry has been "cleaned up" through close state regulation and the transition of casino ownership from private mob control to publicly traded corporations under the scrutiny of a variety of government agencies. This has made it more difficult for criminal syndicates to invest in casinos and for casinos to run dishonest games. Second, high-speed jet plane travel has brought Nevada closer to the rest of the country. Third, the interstate highway system has made Nevada more accessible, especially to the population centers of California. And fourth, the tourism/travel industry has actively promoted Nevada as a vacation destination resort.

In 1976, New Jersey legalized casino gambling in Atlantic City, and the first casino opened in 1978. During the 1950s Cuba was a popular gambling destination for people from New York and the Middle Atlantic states, but the Cuban Revolution of 1958 ended that option. Atlantic City casinos became a convenient, if less exotic, option for East Coast casino gamblers.

The 1960s saw the first legal lotteries in the twentieth century. Beginning with New Hampshire in 1964, fourteen states were operating lotteries by the end of the 1970s. Like casino gambling, the recent growth of lotteries is part of the explosion of gambling that the United States has been experiencing since the 1970s. Both of these topics are treated in greater detail in chapter 4.

Gambling in Other Societies

The recent growth of legalized gambling is not just an American phenomenon. It has been occurring worldwide. This section provides a summary of the availability and popularity of legal gambling in other regions of the world. The close proximity of Canada and Mexico to the United States makes them of special interest.

Canada

Legal gambling can be found in all ten of Canada's provinces. Since Canada's population is concentrated along the northern border of the United States, and given the ease of travel back and forth across the U.S.–Canada border, gambling available in Canada (in particular, casinos in the 1990s) is gambling available to residents of the United States. Table 3.1 presents a summary of the kinds of gambling available.

All Canadian provinces have a lottery, and most of them were developed in the 1980s. As U.S. border states legalized lotteries, provincial governments saw Canadian dollars moving across the border, so they developed their own lotteries to keep the money at home. In 1996, total lottery sales in Canada were $6.98 billion ($1.00 Canadian = $0.70 U.S.). Provincial government profits are used for a variety of purposes, including health services, education, recreation, promotion of tourism, economic development, support of charities, and to increase general revenues.

Every province also has pari-mutuel racing. In Canada, racing is limited to thoroughbred horse and harness racing. There is no greyhound dog racing. In 1996, the total handle (the amount of money wagered) on pari-mutuel racing was $1.77 billion (Canadian).

Charitable gambling is also legal in every province. In most cases quasi-permanent casinos operate on a nearly continuous basis with the charity changing from time to time. In Manitoba, these establishments became so popular that the provincial government decided to license permanent casinos.

TABLE 3.1   Legal Gambling in Canada (May 1997)

Province	Lottery	Pari-Mutuel Racing	Charities (Bingo, Raffles)	Casinos
Alberta	Yes	Yes (4)	Yes	No
British Columbia	Yes	Yes (5)	Yes	Yes
Manitoba	Yes	Yes (2)	Yes	Yes (3)
New Brunswick	Yes	Yes (4)	Yes	No
Newfoundland	Yes	Yes (1)	Yes	No
Nova Scotia	Yes	Yes (3)	Yes	Yes (2)
Ontario	Yes	Yes (18)	Yes	Yes (4)
Prince Edward Island	Yes	Yes (2)	Yes	No
Quebec	Yes	Yes (4)	Yes	Yes (2)
Saskatchewan	Yes	Yes (3)	Yes	Yes (1)
Total		46		12

Sources: North American Gaming Report, 1966, pp. S32–S38; North American Gaming Report, 1997, pp. S32–S38.

Their popularity in British Columbia also led to the creation of a permanent casino that opened in 1997. In 1996, the total handle for charity gambling was $4.57 billion (Canadian).

Six provinces have casinos, all opened since 1993. The casino that has the most impact on the United States is in Windsor, Ontario, across the river from Detroit. It is easily accessed from Detroit (via bridge or tunnel) by car and bus service. The casino has 2,672 slot machines and 117 table games, and averages 16,500 customers per day. The majority of customers come from the United States. The casino's popularity with residents of the Detroit area was a factor in the passage of a referendum in November 1996 to construct three casinos in Detroit. The total handle for Canadian casinos is not available, but total casino revenue in 1996 was $1.1 billion (Canadian).

Casino Niagara, located in Ontario and just across the border from Niagara Falls, New York, will undoubtedly draw customers from New York. During its first twenty-two days of operation, Casino Niagara averaged 20,600 customers per day. It has 2,995 slot machines and 123 table games (*Gaming and Wagering Business,* 1997a).

Canadian casinos differ from their U.S. counterparts in an important way. They are owned and in some cases managed by the provincial governments. In other cases private companies are hired to manage them. Consequently, more of the profits from casinos go to the government than in the United States, where states tax casino revenues between 3 and 20 percent, but private companies own the casinos. Canadian lotteries follow the U.S. model. They are owned by the provinces, but (unlike U.S. state lotteries) they share a portion of their revenues with the federal government. There is also a major difference in how Canada handles gambling winnings. They are not taxed, since governments already are the primary beneficiaries of lotteries (Campbell and Smith, 1998).

Mexico

A broad array of legal gambling activities are available in Mexico, including cock fighting, greyhound and horse racing, jai alai, lottery, football (soccer) pools, and off-track betting. Mexico does not *yet* have casinos. In 1996, however, the national legislature tabled a proposal to legalize up to three casinos in each of six major tourist destination resort areas (including Cancun, Puerto Villarta, and Acapulco). The casinos would target the American, Canadian, and European tourists who have popularized these resort areas in recent years (Doocey, 1997a). In October 1997, an interior ministry official indicated that the government would postpone dealing with this issue until the year 2000 (DeJuana, 1997).

Europe

Legal gambling is pervasive throughout Europe. There are some differences between western and eastern Europe, however. Legal gambling is generally less available in eastern Europe. Table 3.2 presents an overview of the main forms of gambling in European countries, which includes casinos, lotteries, pari-mutuel betting on dog and horse races, off-track betting, and bingo.

With regard to lotteries, a note of clarification is needed. The category "Lotteries" refers to general lotteries, that is, regularly scheduled drawings of numbers for large prizes. Many of the countries that have general lotteries also have instant (scratch off or pull tab) games and betting on soccer pools managed by the lottery. Some of the countries listed as "No" in the lottery column of tables 3.2, 3.3, 3.4, and 3.5 may operate instant games and soccer pools even though they do not have a general lottery.

While the total sales of state lotteries in the United States are the highest of any country in the world ($42.9 billion in 1996), European countries also rank high in total lottery sales. Six of the ten largest lotteries (based on total sales in 1995) are in Germany, Great Britain, Ireland, Spain, France, and Italy (McQueen, 1996).

24

TABLE 3.2   Legal Gambling in Europe (October 1996)

Country	Casinos	Lottery	Dog Racing	Horse Racing	Off Track Betting	Bingo
Northern Europe						
Great Britain	Yes	Yes	Yes	Yes	Yes	Yes
Ireland	No	Yes	Yes	Yes	Yes	Yes
Denmark	Yes	Yes	Yes	Yes	Yes	No
Finland	Yes	Yes	No	Yes	Yes	Yes
Iceland	No	Yes	No	No	No	Yes
Norway	No	Yes	No	Yes	Yes	No
Sweden	No	Yes	No	Yes	Yes	No
Western/Central Europe						
Austria	Yes	Yes	No	Yes	Yes	No
Belgium	Yes	Yes	Yes	Yes	Yes	No
France	Yes	Yes	No	Yes	Yes	No
Germany	Yes	Yes	No	Yes	Yes	No
Luxemburg	Yes	Yes	No	No	No	No
Monaco	Yes	No	No	No	No	No
Netherlands	Yes	Yes	No	Yes	Yes	Yes
Switzerland	Yes	Yes	No	Yes	Yes	No
Southern Europe						
Cyprus	Yes	Yes	No	Yes	No	No
Gibraltar	Yes	Yes	No	No	No	Yes
Greece	Yes	Yes	No	Yes	Yes	No
Italy	Yes	Yes	Yes	Yes	Yes	No
Macedonia	Yes	Yes	No	No	No	No
Madieira	Yes	Yes	No	No	No	No
Malta	Yes	Yes	No	Yes	No	Yes
Portugal	Yes	Yes	No	No	No	Yes
Spain	Yes	Yes	Yes	Yes	Yes	Yes

(continued)

TABLE 3.2   (continued)

Country	Casinos	Lottery	Dog Racing	Horse Racing	Off Track Betting	Bingo
Eastern Europe						
Albania	No	Yes	No	No	No	No
Bulgaria	Yes	Yes	No	Yes	Yes	No
Croatia	Yes	Yes	No	No	No	No
Czech Republic	Yes	Yes	Yes	Yes	Yes	No
Estonia	Yes	Yes	No	No	No	No
Hungary	Yes	Yes	No	Yes	Yes	No
Latvia	Yes	Yes	No	No	No	No
Lithuania	Yes	Yes	No	No	No	No
Poland	Yes	Yes	No	Yes	Yes	No
Romania	Yes	Yes	No	Yes	Yes	No
Russia	Yes	Yes	No	Yes	Yes	No
Slovakia	Yes	Yes	No	Yes	No	No
Slovenia	Yes	No	No	No	No	No
Yugoslavia	Yes	Yes	No	Yes	No	Yes

Note: The category "Lotteries" refers to general lotteries, that is, regularly scheduled drawings of numbers for large prizes. Some of the countries listed as "No" in the "Lotteries" column may operate instant games and soccer pools even though they do not have a general lottery.
Source: Adapted with permission from Patricia A. McQueen, 1996, "World Gaming at a Glance," *Gaming and Wagering Business,* 17, Nr. 10, pp. 80–84.

Great Britain and Spain offer the greatest variety of gambling opportunities—all the major types of gambling (casino, lottery, dog and horse racing, OTB, and bingo) are available. The Netherlands, Finland, (everything but dog racing), Denmark, and Belgium (everything but bingo) rank next. Of the thirty-eight European countries included in table 3.3, only five do *not* have legal casinos. Two of these are Scandinavian countries—Norway and Sweden. Clearly, casino gambling is pervasive in European countries.

Every European country except Monaco and Slovenia has lotteries. In the case of Monaco, this probably reflects the fact that casinos are a major industry and a lottery would simply compete with what is one of the country's major industries. Dog racing is not common in western Europe. Only seven countries have it. Its scarcity in eastern Europe is particularly noticeable—only Yugoslavia has dog racing. Bingo is available in northern, central, and southern Europe, but in eastern Europe only Yugoslavia has legalized this form of gambling.

A final generalization is that the majority of countries that have legalized dog and/or horse racing also have legalized off-track betting. The only exceptions to this are Cyprus, Malta, Yugoslavia, and Slovakia, which have some form of racing, but do not have off-track betting.

European casinos differ from those in the United States in several ways. Most importantly, they typically are owned by some unit of government. Even when casinos are privately owned, the government may own the building housing the casino and play a larger role in casino operations than is the case in the United States. In some cases taxation rates on privately owned and operated casinos are so high that government is the primary beneficiary if not the "de facto" owner. For example, gross revenue taxation rates are 93 percent in Germany, 80 percent in France, 60 percent in Austria, and 54 percent in Spain (Thompson, 1998).

In addition, casinos tend to be smaller and more sedate than their U.S. (or Canadian) counterparts. A casino with fifteen to twenty table games and several hundred machine games would be large. They also tend to operate as local monopolies, usually only one per community. European casinos serve a local clientele and are not licensed and developed with the idea of attracting travelers and tourists as is the case in the United States (especially Nevada and Atlantic City).

The hours of operation of European casinos are more limited than in the United States; typically, they are open only in the evening. They usually cannot advertise, and the sale of alcohol is severely restricted. The nongambling forms of entertainment associated with casinos in the United States are virtually nonexistent. Overall, they are a different phenomenon than one finds in the United States (Thompson, 1998).

South America, Central America, and the Caribbean

An overview of legal gambling in South America, Central America, and the Caribbean is presented in table 3.3. Several generalizations can be made. Gambling on cockfights is fairly common in this region of the world. Fourteen of the forty-one countries in table 3.3 have legal cockfight gambling. The lottery is the most common form of gambling, and all but seven of these countries have a general lottery. Bingo is found throughout the countries in this region: more than half have legal gambling on bingo.

Dog racing is not common in this region and only the Dominican Republic currently has gambling on dog races. Horse racing is another

TABLE 3.3   Legal Gambling in South America, Central America, and the Caribbean (October 1996)

Country	Casinos	Lotteries	Dog Racing	Horse Racing	Off-Track Betting	Bingo	Cock-fighting
South America							
Argentina	Yes	Yes	No	Yes	Yes	Yes	No
Bolivia	No	Yes	No	No	No	Yes	No
Brazil	No	Yes	No	Yes	No	Yes	Yes
Chile	Yes	Yes	No	No	No	No	No
Colombia	Yes	Yes	No	Yes	Yes	Yes	Yes
Ecuador	Yes	Yes	No	Yes	Yes	Yes	Yes
Guyana	No	Yes	No	Yes	Yes	Yes	No
Paraguay	Yes	Yes	No	No	No	Yes	Yes
Peru	Yes	Yes	No	Yes	No	No	Yes
Surinam	Yes	Yes	No	Yes	No	Yes	No
Uruguay	Yes	Yes	No	Yes	No	Yes	No
Venezuela	Yes	Yes	No	Yes	Yes	Yes	No
Central America							
Belize	No	No	No	No	No	No	No
Costa Rica	Yes	Yes	No	No	No	Yes	No
El Salvador	No	No	No	No	No	No	No
Guatemala	No	Yes	No	Yes	No	Yes	No
Honduras	Yes	Yes	No	No	No	Yes	Yes
Mexico	No	Yes	Yes	Yes	Yes	No	Yes
Nicaragua	No*	Yes	No	No	No	Yes	No
Panama	Yes	Yes	No	Yes	Yes	No	Yes
Caribbean							
Antigua	Yes	Yes	No	Yes	Yes	Yes	No
Aruba	Yes	Yes	No	Yes	No	Yes	Yes
Bahamas	Yes	Yes	No	No	No	No	No
Barbados	No	Yes	No*	Yes	Yes	Yes	No
Bonaire	Yes	No	No	No	No	No	No

(continued)

28

TABLE 3.3 (continued)

Country	Casinos	Lotteries	Dog Racing	Horse Racing	Off-Track Betting	Bingo	Cock-fighting
Curacao	Yes	Yes	No	No	No	Yes	No
Dominica	No	No*	No	No	No	No	No
Dominican Republic	Yes	Yes	Yes	Yes	Yes	No	Yes
Grenada	No	No	No	No*	No	No	No*
Guadeloupe	Yes	Yes	No	Yes	No	Yes	Yes
Haiti	Yes	Yes	No*	No	No	No	Yes
Jamaica	No	Yes	No	Yes	Yes	Yes	No
Martinique	Yes	Yes	No	Yes	No	Yes	Yes
Netherlands Antilles	No	Yes	No	No	No	No	No
Puerto Rico	Yes	Yes	No	Yes	Yes	Yes	Yes
St. Kitts	Yes	No	No	No	No	Yes	No
St. Lucia	Yes	Yes	No	No	No	Yes	No
St. Maarten	Yes	Yes	No	No	No	No	No
St. Vincent	Yes	No	No	No	No	Yes	No
Trinidad and Tobago	No	Yes	No	Yes	No	No	No
U.S. Virgin Islands	No	Yes	No	Yes	No	No	No

Note: The category "Lotteries" refers to general lotteries, that is, regularly scheduled drawings of numbers for large prizes. Some of the countries listed as "No" in the "Lotteries" column may operate instant games and soccer pools even though they do not have a general lottery.
*Previously operational but not operational now.
Source: Adapted with permission from McQueen, 1996b.

matter, however. More than half of these countries have gambling on horse races and of these, more than half also have off-track betting.

Casino gambling is pervasive throughout South America and in the Caribbean. It is less common in the Central American nations. Nearly two-thirds of these countries have casinos. In the Caribbean, casinos are an integral part of the tourism industry and are typically operated by resort hotels catering to North American and European tourists. In some Caribbean nations, nationals are not permitted to gamble in the casinos. They exist strictly as places for tourist dollars to be left behind.

Africa

While some form of legal gambling exists in the majority of African nations, there is much less variety in the types of gambling available than there is in the United States and the regions of the world discussed thus far. As can be seen in table 3.4, bingo and dog racing are found in only a few countries. Sixteen of these thirty-nine countries have horse racing and half of those sixteen also have off-track betting.

TABLE 3.4   Legal Gambling in Africa (October 1996)

Country	Casinos	Lotteries	Dog Racing	Horse Racing	Off Track Betting	Bingo
Northern Africa						
Algeria	No	Yes	No	Yes	No	No*
Benin	Yes	Yes	No	No	No	No
Burkina Faso	No	Yes	No	No	No	No
Cameroon	Yes	Yes	No	No	No	No
Cape Verde	No	No*	No	No	No	No
Central African Republic	Yes	Yes	No	No	No	No
Chad	No	No	No	Yes	No	No
Egypt	Yes	No	No	Yes	No	No
Ethiopia	Yes	Yes	No	No	No	No
Gambia	Yes	No	No	No	No	No
Ghana	Yes	Yes	No	Yes	No	No
Guinea-Bissau	No	No	No	No	No	No
Ivory Coast	Yes	Yes	No	No	No	No
Liberia	Yes	Yes	No	No	No	No
Mali	No	Yes	No	No	No	No
Morocco	Yes	Yes	No	Yes	Yes	No
Niger	Yes	Yes	No	No	No	No
Nigeria	Yes	No	No	Yes	No	No
Senegal	Yes	Yes	No	Yes	No	No
Sierra Leone	Yes	No	No	No	No	No
Togo	Yes	Yes	No	No	No	No
Tunisia	Yes	Yes	No	Yes	Yes	No

(continued)

TABLE 3.4 (continued)

Country	Casinos	Lotteries	Dog Racing	Horse Racing	Off Track Betting	Bingo
Southern Africa						
Angola	No	Yes	No	No	No	No
Botswana	Yes	No	Yes	Yes	Yes	Yes
Burundi	No	Yes	Yes	Yes	Yes	No
Congo	Yes	Yes	No	No	No	No
Gabon	Yes	Yes	No	No	No	No
Kenya	Yes	Yes	No	Yes	No	No
Lesotho	Yes	No	No	Yes	No	No
Madagascar	Yes	Yes	No	Yes	Yes	No
Mozambique	No	Yes	No	No	No	No
Namibia	Yes	No	No	No	No	No
South Africa	Yes	Yes	No	Yes	Yes	No
Swaziland	Yes	No	No	No	No	No
Tanzania	Yes	Yes	No	No	No	No
Uganda	Yes	No*	No	No	No	No
Zaire	Yes	No	No	No	No	No
Zambia	Yes	No	No	Yes	Yes	Yes
Zimbabwe	Yes	Yes	No	Yes	Yes	Yes

Note: The category "Lotteries" refers to general lotteries, that is, regularly scheduled drawings of numbers for large prizes. Some of the countries listed as "No" in the "Lotteries" column may operate instant games and soccer pools even though they do not have a general lottery.
*Previously operational but not operational now.
Source: Adapted with permission from McQueen, 1996b.

Casinos and lotteries are much more common. A little over three-quarters of the countries of Africa have legal casino gambling, and almost two-thirds have lotteries. Lotteries are more common in the northern part of the continent, while casinos are more common in the nations of southern Africa.

In the nation of South Africa, gambling has been growing at a high rate and is expected to rise dramatically in the near future.

A nation of 40 million people, South Africa has seventeen legal casinos. But national legislation passed in 1995 (the "National Gambling

Bill") authorized the licensing of forty casinos. Other legislation has authorized the creation of a national lottery. In addition, there are an estimated two thousand to three thousand illegal slot clubs, which the 1995 legislation sought to eliminate through the creation of legal casinos. It is expected that casinos will be located in and near major urban areas and in destination resort developments that will offer (in a manner similar to Las Vegas) casino gambling as part of a broad resort entertainment menu.

In 1995, South Africa's seventeen casinos generated gross revenues of between R3 billion and R4.5 billion (1 Rand = $0.26 U.S.). According to some estimates, gross revenues from casino gambling could total R7.5 billion annually by 2021.

The legalization of casinos was a response to the popularity of the (untaxed) illegal slot clubs and the fact that South Africans had been spending money outside the country in casinos in neighboring Namibia, Botswana, Lesotho, Swaziland, and Mozambique (Doocey, 1997b). The legalization of gambling is, in part, a strategy to keep the money at home.

Asia and the Middle East

Of the forty countries listed in table 3.5, only six have none of these major types of legal gambling. These are the Asian countries of Indonesia, Pakistan, and Taiwan and the Middle Eastern countries of Iran, Iraq, and the United Arab Emirates. None of the Middle Eastern countries have bingo or dog racing, and only Turkey has horse racing. While bingo and dog racing exist in some Asian countries, less than one-quarter have bingo and only 16 percent have dog racing.

Over half of the countries listed in table 3.5 have casino gambling, and nearly two-thirds have lotteries. While some of the Asian countries are small island nations that have developed casinos as part of their tourism industries, others have developed casinos primarily for the resident population. Macau stands out as a special case of a very small country with an enormous casino industry that attracts visitors from throughout Asia.

Like South Africa, Australia's gambling industry—especially casinos—has experienced tremendous growth in recent years. In fact, nowhere in the world has gambling been booming the way it has in Australia, where pari-mutuel betting, lotteries, and fourteen casinos exist. In June of 1996, there were 134,000 slot and video poker machines in casinos, private clubs, hotels, and taverns, and the number is expected to increase to 189,000 by the year 2000. Australia's casinos also have 1,076 table games (*Gaming and Wagering Business,* 1997b). In 1996, the per capita handle was $900 ($1.00 Australian = $0.78 U.S.). By the year 2000 it is expected to hit $950 ($700 U.S.).

TABLE 3.5 Legal Gambling in Asia and the Middle East (October 1996)

Country	Casinos	Lotteries	Dog Racing	Horse Racing	Off Track Betting	Bingo
Asia						
Australia	Yes	Yes	Yes	Yes	Yes	Yes
Bhutan	No	Yes	No	No	No	No
Burma	Yes	No	No	No	No	No
Cambodia	Yes	Yes	No	No	No	No
China	Yes	Yes	No	Yes	No	No
Fiji	No	No	No	Yes	Yes	No
Guam	No	Yes	Yes	No	No	Yes
Hong Kong	No	Yes	No	Yes	Yes	No
India	Yes	Yes	No	Yes	No	No
Indonesia	No*	No*	No*	No*	No	No
Japan	No	Yes	No	Yes	Yes	No
Laos	Yes	No	No	No	No	No
Macau	Yes	Yes	Yes	Yes	Yes	No
Malaysia	Yes	Yes	No	Yes	No	No
Mauritius	Yes	Yes	No	Yes	Yes	No
Nepal	Yes	No	No	Yes	No	Yes
New Caledonia	Yes	No	No	No	No	No
New Zealand	Yes	Yes	Yes	Yes	Yes	Yes
Northern Mariana Islands	No	Yes	No	No	No	No
Pakistan	No	No	No	No	No	No
Papua New Guinea	No	Yes	No	Yes	Yes	Yes
Philippines	Yes	Yes	No	Yes	No*	Yes
Seychelles	Yes	No	No	No	No	No
Singapore	Yes	Yes	Yes	Yes	Yes	Yes
South Korea	Yes	Yes	No	Yes	No	No
Sri Lanka	No*	Yes	No	No*	No	No
Taiwan	No	No	No	No	No	No
Thailand	No	Yes	No	Yes	No	No
Tinian	Yes	No	No	No	No	No

(continued)

33

TABLE 3.5 (continued)

Country	Casinos	Lotteries	Dog Racing	Horse Racing	Off Track Betting	Bingo
Vanuatu	Yes	Yes	No	No	No	No
Vietnam	Yes	Yes	No	Yes	No	No
Middle East						
Afghanistan	No	Yes	No	No	No	No
Iran	No*	No	No	No*	No	No
Iraq	No	No	No	No	No	No
Israel	No	Yes	No	No	No	No
Jordan	No	Yes	No	No	No	No
Lebanon	Yes	Yes	No	No	No	No
Syria	Yes	No	No	No	No	No
Turkey	Yes	Yes	No	Yes	Yes	No
United Arab Emirates	No*	No	No	No	No	No

Note: The category "Lotteries" refers to general lotteries,that is, regularly scheduled drawings of numbers for large prizes. Some of the countries listed as "No" in the "Lotteries" column may operate instant games and soccer pools even though they do not have a general lottery.
*Previously operational but not operational now.
Source: Adapted with permission from McQueen, 1996b.

Summary

Gambling, both legal and illegal, has been popular throughout American history. It has been permitted and encouraged at certain times and prohibited and discouraged at others. Governments have consistently turned to gambling, mainly in the form of lotteries, to raise revenues and respond to fiscal crises. History demonstrates an ambivalence toward the desirability and appropriateness of gambling. Illegal gambling—particularly numbers games and casinos—has also flourished, especially when legal forms have not been available.

The United States is by no means alone with regard to the popularity of gambling. The growth of most forms of gambling in Canada has paralleled their growth in the United States. Australia and South Africa stand out as nations where legalized gambling is growing rapidly. Many European nations exceed the United States in the variety and availability of legal gambling. Gambling has also developed in many other parts of the world (the Caribbean, Asia) where economic development strategies are partly based on tourism.

Chapter 4

Recent Growth of the Gambling Industry

Until the early 1960s, legal gambling outside the state of Nevada was limited largely to horse and dog racing and charitable bingo. By the end of 1993, forty-eight states and the District of Columbia had legalized gambling of some kind. Only Hawaii and Utah did not, and still do not, have legal gambling.

Legal gambling is big business. In 1974, $17.3 billion was legally wagered (Commission 1976). During the eight years from 1974 to 1982, the amount of money legally wagered increased more than sevenfold to $125.8 billion. Between 1982 and 1996, the total amount of money wagered annually increased by 366 percent. Table 4.1 presents a summary overview of the growth (and in a few cases, decline) of different segments of the legal gambling industry in the United States from 1982 to 1996.

Handle

A number of interesting trends can be identified, and comparisons can be made, using the data in table 4.1. The Grand Total at the bottom of the table shows the total handle for all the forms of gambling presented in the table. It can also be thought of as the annual average for the gambling industry. The handle increased substantially from 1982 to 1996, although there was minimal growth between 1990 and 1991. During the fifteen year period, 1982 to 1996, the total handle grew by 366 percent (last column in the table) or an average of a little over twenty-four percent per year.

Pari-Mutuels

While the entire gambling industry has grown substantially, not all segments have participated in this growth. The pari-mutuel segment (horse and dog racing and jai alai) has lagged behind the rest of the industry and the handle at horse and dog tracks actually declined between 1982 and 1996. The

**TABLE 4.1   Gross Annual Handle, 1982–1996
(billions of dollars)**

	1982	1990	1991	1992	1993	1994	1995	1996	Percentage Change 1982–1996
Pari-mutuels									
Horses									
Tracks	10.0	10.4	9.9	9.5	8.9	5.6	4.7	4.0	−60
OTB	1.7	3.7	4.0	4.6	4.9	4.2	5.0	4.8	+182
ITW[c]	—	—	—	—	—	4.3	5.2	6.0	+40
Total*	11.7	14.1	13.9	14.1	13.7	14.2	14.7	15.0	+28
Greyhounds									
Tracks	2.2	3.4	3.5	3.2	3.2	2.4	2.0	1.5	−32
OTB[c]	—	a	a	a	a	0.1	0.1	0.1	0
ITW[c]	—	—	—	—	—	0.5	0.6	0.7	+40
Total*	2.2	3.5	3.5	3.3	3.3	3.0	2.8	2.3	+5
Jai Alai	0.6	0.5	0.5	0.4	0.4	0.3	0.2	0.2	−67
Total for Pari-Mutuels*	14.5	18.2	17.9	17.8	17.4	17.4	17.8	17.5	+21
Lotteries									
Traditional Games	4.1	20.7	20.6	23.0	27.0	30.0	32.5	33.9	+727
Video Lotteries[d]	—	0.3	0.4	1.3	3.9	4.4	6.4	9.0	+2,900
Total Lotteries*	4.1	21.0	21.0	24.4	30.9	34.5	38.9	42.9	+946
Casinos									
Nevada/ New Jersey Slots	14.4	76.2	84.4	94.6	102.6	113.0	121.3	126.8	+780
Nevada/ New Jersey Tables	87.0	161.6	149.7	143.1	150.9	170.8	185.6	178.7	+105
Cruise Ships[b,d]	—	3.7	4.1	4.3	4.5	5.1	5.8	6.1	+65
Riverboats[e]	—	—	1.1	7.3	27.1	63.8	88.1	104.4	+9,391
Landbased and Other[d]	—	0.7	1.1	3.6	12.2	15.1	21.8	22.6	+3,128
Total Casinos*	101.4	242.2	240.4	252.9	297.3	367.9	422.6	438.7	+333

(continued)

TABLE 4.1 (continued)

	1982	1990	1991	1992	1993	1994	1995	1996	Percent-age Change 1982–1996
Bookmaking									
Sports	0.4	1.7	1.9	1.8	2.0	2.1	2.4	2.5	+525
Horse	0.1	0.5	0.4	0.3	0.2	0.5	0.2	0.1	+0
Total Books*	0.5	2.2	2.3	2.1	2.2	2.7	2.6	2.6	+420
Card Rooms	1.0	8.4	8.4	8.4	8.4	9.3	9.7	9.8	+880
Charity Bingo	3.0	4.1	4.2	4.3	4.2	4.2	4.1	4.0	+33
Other Charity Games	1.2	4.5	4.5	4.8	4.9	5.0	5.7	5.7	+375
Indian Reservations									
Bingo[d]	—	1.3	1.4	1.4	1.4	1.5	1.6	2.1	+62
Casinos[d]	—	1.3	4.0	13.7	27.5	39.6	47.4	63.1	+4,754
Total Indian Reservations*[d]	—	2.6	5.4	15.2	29.0	41.1	49.0	65.2	+2,408
*Grand Total**	125.8	303.1	304.1	329.9	394.3	482.1	550.4	586.5	+366

Notes:
*In some cases figures in columns will not add to the total because of rounding error.
— Indicates data not available or activity did not exist.
a. Less than $0.1 billion.
b. Figures for 1995 and 1996 include "cruises to nowhere."
c. Change from 1994 to 1996.
d. Change from 1990 to 1996.
e. Change from 1991 to 1996.
Sources: E. M. Christiansen et al., "1991 Gross Annual Wager, Part I: Handle," *Gaming and Wagering Business,* 13, no. 7 (July 15, 1992–August 14, 1992): 25; E. M. Christiansen and P. A. McQueen, "1992 Gross Annual Wager, Part I: Handle," *Gaming and Wagering Business,* 14, no. 7 (July 15, 1993–August 14, 1993): 12; E. M. Christiansen et al., "1993 Gross Annual Wager," *Gaming and Wagering Business,* 15, no. 8 (August 5, 1994): 17; E. M. Christiansen et al., "1994 Gross Annual Wager," *Gaming and Wagering Business,* 16, no. 8 (August 1995): 32; E. M. Christiansen et al., "1995 Gross Annual Wager," *Gaming and Wagering Business,* 17, no. 8 (August 1996): 60; E. M. Christiansen et al., "1996 Gross Annual Wager," *Gaming and Wagering Business,* 18, no. 8 (August 1997): 8.

total pari-mutuel handle of $17.5 billion in 1996 accounted for only 2.9 percent of the American gambling industry's handle of $586.5 billion.

As of September 1996, twenty-four states had legalized off-track betting (OTB) facilities. It is much more common for bets to be taken on horse races than on dog races. In 1995 and 1996, more money was bet on horse races at OTBs than at tracks.

Handle. The gross amount of money wagered at any form of gambling. Handle can be used to refer to money wagered over a particular period of time or on a specific event. For example, it can be the total amount of money wagered on all forms of gambling during a period of time such as a year or a week, or it can be the amount wagered on one race at a particular racetrack. In different accounting systems, handle is synonymous with gross wagering, betting, gross betting, gross amount bet, money staked, turnover, and lottery sales. Handle is viewed as a measure of the total volume of wagering activity. For example, if a person bets $2 on a horse race and wins $10, and then bets that $10 on the next five races without winning anything, the handle would be $12 (the original $2 bet and the $10 won), even though the amount lost was only the original $2 bet.

Drop. In casino accounting, the cash exchanged for chips and risked against the casino. It is also referred to as the player's "bankroll."

Use of "Handle" and "Drop." Casinos report handle for slot and video-poker machines since the amount of money wagered can be identified. However, at table games (blackjack, craps, roulette, baccarat, etc.) it is not possible to identify handle, so drop is used instead.

Hold Percentage. The ratio of win to drop for table games. Table games typically hold (i.e., win from the players) 12 to 20 percent of drop, depending on the game and the players' choices. For machine games, the hold is the difference between the handle and the amount of money paid out (i.e., the casino's win).

Hold and House Advantage. It is easy to confuse hold percentages and the house or casino advantage for table games. The house advantage is the expected value for table games stated as a percent of handle, not drop. These advantages are built into the structure and rules of the game. For example, in Nevada and Atlantic City, the house advantage for roulette is 5.26 percent (except for one bet, where the house advantage is 7.89 percent), 1.402 percent on the "Don't Pass" line at craps, 1 to 1.2 percent for baccarat, and so on.

Relationship Between Handle, Drop, and Win. These relationships can best be explained with an example. Suppose that a player buys a hundred $1 chips and bets them one at a time at a table game that has a house advantage of 1 percent. The average player, winning some bets

> and losing others, will generate a *handle* of $10,000 before the $100 *drop* (or bankroll) is lost. This results in a $100 *win* for the casino.
>
> *Gross Gambling Revenues (GGR).* The handle minus payouts, prizes, or winnings returned to players. From the perspective of the operators of a commercial game, GGR is the money collectively extracted from the players and transferred to the operators of the game. From the perspective of players, it is the cost of playing the game. Taxes imposed by governments are typically based on GGR. In different accounting systems, win, takeout, retention, and net receipts are used as synonyms for GGR.

Inter-track wagering (ITW) occurs when people at one track bet on televised races being run at other tracks. Some states permit inter-track wagering only on races being run within the state (intrastate ITW), while others permit wagering on races occurring in other states (interstate ITW). As of September 1996, forty-two states had legalized interstate ITW and thirty-four had legalized intrastate ITW (McQueen, 1996: 52–56). By permitting inter-track wagering, many states without OTBs have, in effect, created a kind of off-track betting opportunity.

Clearly, the OTB and ITW handle has been increasing and has offset the decline in handle at tracks. Without OTBs and ITW, the handle of the horse and dog racing segment would be substantially lower than it is.

Lotteries

State operated lotteries have experienced substantial growth. The first lottery in this century began in 1964 in New Hampshire, following a decade of legislative efforts to establish a lottery. By 1980, fourteen states had lotteries (Clotfelter and Cook, 1989). At the end of 1996, thirty-seven states and the District of Columbia had lotteries or were participating in multi-state lotteries (Christiansen, 1997).

The handle for "traditional" lottery games (weekly and daily drawings, scratch-off and pull-tab games) has grown at almost twice the rate of the overall gambling industry. Video lottery games, relatively new to the gambling scene, have enjoyed a steady growth since the early 1990s. In 1996, total lottery sales accounted for 7.3 percent of the gambling industry's total handle.

An overview of the spread of lotteries is presented in table 4.2. Two things are noteworthy in this table. First, it is apparent that lotteries have

TABLE 4.2 The Growth of Lotteries in the United States, 1964–1996

Jurisdiction	Year Established	Jurisdiction	Year Established
New Hampshire	1964	Iowa	1985
New York	1967	California	1985
New Jersey	1970	West Virginia	1986
Connecticut	1972	Missouri	1986
Massachusetts	1972	Kansas	1987
Pennsylvania	1972	South Dakota	1987
Michigan	1972	Montana	1987
Maryland	1973	Florida	1988
Rhode Island	1974	Virginia	1988
Maine	1974	Wisconsin	1988
Illinois	1974	Idaho	1989
Ohio	1974	Indiana	1989
Delaware	1975	Kentucky	1989
Vermont	1978	Minnesota	1990
Arizona	1981	Louisiana	1991
District of Columbia	1982	Texas	1992
Washington	1982	Georgia	1993
Colorado	1983	Nebraska	1994
Oregon	1985	New Mexico	1996

Sources: "30 Years of Lottery Success," Supplement, *Gaming and Wagering Business,* March 5, 1994; E. M. Christiansen, "1996 Gross Annual Wager," *Gaming and Wagering Business,* 18, no. 7 (August): 20.

been initiated in "bursts." After the New Hampshire lottery started, six years passed before there were two more. However, during the next five years, ten more were started. During the decade of the 1980s, eighteen more states started lotteries. The table also reveals that there was a pattern of lotteries spreading to adjacent or nearby states. This "copycat" effect was apparent early on. After the New Hampshire lottery started, the next four lotteries were initiated by neighboring states. This pattern can also be seen in the case of Illinois and Ohio (1974), Missouri and Kansas (1986–87), South Dakota and Montana (1987), Indiana and Kentucky (1989), and Louisiana and Texas (1991–92). When legislators believe that residents of their state are spending money on lotteries in adjacent or nearby states, they start a lottery to "keep the money at home."

Several factors are involved in the spread of lotteries since the early 1960s. To begin with, pro-gambling sentiments had been strong for decades, and the popularity of illegal numbers games suggested that people wanted to gamble, even if it meant involvement with organized crime. State lotteries created a legal way for people to continue playing the numbers. In effect, lotteries are the legal version of the numbers game, run by the state rather than by criminals. Seven national opinion polls conducted between 1938 and 1964 found that 48 to 54 percent of the respondents favored a state or federal lottery to raise money for everything from increasing general revenues to reducing the national debt. Between 1960 and 1980, when voters had the opportunity to vote on whether or not their state should have a lottery, those voting in favor ranged from a low of 42 percent (North Dakota) to a high of 81 percent (New Jersey).

The spread of lotteries was also helped by the fact that those in New Hampshire, New York, New Jersey, Connecticut, Massachusetts, and so on were free of the fraud and corruption that had soured the nation on lotteries a century earlier.

Lotteries were seen by state legislators—and sold to the public—as an alternative to raising taxes. Viewed as a voluntary tax, revenues from state lotteries were earmarked for different purposes, including funding educational programs, programs for the elderly, and property tax relief. Many legislators preferred to vote for a lottery rather than face reelection after voting for higher taxes.

Finally, the public's acceptance of lotteries and gambling in general is part of a broader liberalization of attitudes on a wide range of social issues since the 1960s. Support for lotteries and acceptance of gambling as a recreational activity need to be seen as part of the trend involving changing attitudes toward divorce, abortion, women's rights, premarital sex, homosexuality, and racial integration.

Casinos

Casinos are the largest single sector of the gambling industry. From 1982 to 1996, the percentage increase for casino gambling was only slightly below that for the overall gambling industry (333 percent compared to 366 percent). In 1996, 74.8 percent of the industry handle was wagered in non-Indian reservation casinos. If Indian reservation casinos were included, casino gambling would account for 85.6 percent of the total industry handle.

Nevada and Atlantic City

Nevada and Atlantic City are the major gambling centers within the casino industry. (Table 4.1 presents data on these venues by combining the handle for slots and table games in these two locations.) Although table games in Nevada and New Jersey have a larger handle than slots, the difference has been narrowing since 1982. Slots have been growing as a source of handle and from 1982 to 1996, the percentage increase was 7.4 times larger than the handle increase for table games. As new gamblers less experienced with table games have come to participate in gambling, the expansion of casino gambling in Nevada and Atlantic City has resulted in the increased popularity of machine games.

In 1996, the casino handle for Nevada ($114.1 billion) was almost three times the size of the casino handle for Atlantic City ($39.3 billion). Atlantic City had 12 casinos while Nevada had 383. Nevada had 169,323 slot machines compared to 31,494 in Atlantic City. And Atlantic City had only 1,376 table games compared to 5,199 in Nevada. While Atlantic City is a major gambling destination for residents of Philadelphia, the New York City metropolitan area, and the mid-Atlantic states, Nevada is the premier casino gambling venue in the United States, drawing customers from throughout the nation and the world (*Gaming and Wagering Business* 1997).

Riverboat/Waterborne/Dockside Casinos

Riverboat and other waterborne casinos are an important recent development in the gambling industry. These gambling venues include Indiana vessels on Lake Michigan and "dockside" casinos in Mississippi that do not actually cruise anywhere. For simplicity, these are all referred to as "riverboat casinos."

The riverboat casino handle is considerably smaller in absolute dollars than the handles for Atlantic City or Nevada, but it has been growing rapidly in recent years. Riverboats are the fastest growing segment of the gambling industry, with more than a 9,391 percent increase in handle from 1991 to 1996.

Riverboats are a middle American phenomenon. With the exception of Indiana, they operate in states that border the Mississippi River. Table 4.3 presents a summary of riverboat casinos. As of June 1996, sixty-six riverboat casinos were operating in six states. There have been attempts to legalize riverboat casinos in Minnesota, Wisconsin, Ohio, and Pennsylvania, but proposals have failed to make it through the legislative process or have been defeated by voters in referenda.

Other Land-Based Casinos

Land-based casinos operated legally only in Nevada until 1978, when the first casino opened in Atlantic City. In the late 1980s and early 1990s, limited stakes casino gambling was legalized in Deadwood, South Dakota, and Cripple Creek, Central City, and Black Hawk, Colorado. The

TABLE 4.3   Riverboat Casinos, by State (as of June 1996)

State	Number of Casinos	Year Begun	Number of Tables	Number of Slots
Iowa	9	1991	288	5,493
Illinois	13	1991	464	8,193
Mississippi	20	1992	1,233	32,114
Louisiana	12	1993	605	11,337
Missouri	9	1994	617	10,669
Indiana*	6	1995	375	7,126
Total**	69		3,582	74,932

Notes:
*An additional five licenses are authorized for Indiana.
**Through 1998, expansion of existing casinos and construction on new ones are expected to add 8,089 slots and 367 table games.
Sources: "North American Gaming Report, 1996," *Gaming and Wagering Business,* 17, no. 7 (July 1996): S3–S38; "North American Gaming Report, 1994," Supplement, *Gaming and Wagering Business,* July 5, 1994; *Central States Gaming,* 1, no. 14 (June 9, 1995): 5; P. Doocey, "An Overview of Riverboat Gaming: Full Speed Ahead," *Gaming and Wagering Business,* 14, no. 11 (November 15, 1993–December 14, 1993): 1, 38–40; A. Andersen, *Economic Impacts of Casino Gaming in the United States: Volume 1: Macro Study* (Washington, DC: American Gaming Association, 1996); "North American Gaming Report, 1997," *Gaming and Wagering Business,* 18, no. 7 (July 1997): S3–S38.

handle for these venues is small, but these communities are important regional gambling centers. Their popularity is attested to by the substantial increase in handle between 1990 and 1996 (see table 4.1).

Bookmaking and Card Rooms

In 1996, bookmaking (legal wagering at Nevada sports books on horse racing and sporting events) and card rooms represented only 2.1 percent of the total gambling handle. However, they have been growing steadily in recent years. Both of these gambling activities have 1982–1996 growth rates above the overall growth rate for the entire gambling industry.

Card rooms are primarily a California phenomenon, although they are legal in fourteen states. While they can be found throughout the state of California, they are concentrated in the southern part of the state. In 1996, six of the state's ten largest clubs were located in the Los Angeles metropolitan area (Christiansen, 1997: 38).

Although Nevada bookmaking has grown at a strong rate overall, race books (like the racing industry to which they are linked) have not shown steady growth due to several factors. Opportunities to gamble on racing (at tracks, through OTBs and ITWs) have increased throughout the country. Gamblers who come to Nevada are less likely to gamble on something that they can gamble on at home. They are more likely to gamble on something like sporting events, which they cannot legally gamble on elsewhere.

Charity Bingo and Other Charity Games

Charity bingo games are operated by churches, fraternal organizations, and other nonprofit charitable organizations. The category "charity games" refers to casino games operated on behalf of charitable organizations. They are often advertised and promoted as "Casino Nights" or "Las Vegas Nights." They tend to be brief (one night) events. They are not permanent establishments.

As of September 1996, forty-six states and the District of Columbia had legalized charity bingo (only Arkansas, Hawaii, Tennessee, and Utah prohibit this form of gambling). Forty-two states and the District of Columbia have legalized charity games (only Arkansas, Hawaii, Tennessee, Utah, Georgia, Nevada, North Carolina, and South Carolina prohibit charity games). It may seem odd that Nevada has not legalized charitable casino games or a lottery, but to do so would create direct competition with the commercial casino industry. Given the ubiquity of lotteries throughout the country, it also seems unlikely that visitors to Nevada would spend much time and money playing the lottery or charitable casino games when casino games are readily available.

Charity bingo and other charity games are a small portion of the gambling industry. Combined, they had a handle about the same size as that of card rooms in 1996. Charity bingo has experienced modest growth between 1982 and 1996, but other charity games have kept pace with the overall growth rate of the gambling industry.

Indian Reservation Gambling

In October 1988, Congress passed the Indian Gaming Regulatory Act (IGRA). This Act recognized gambling as a means by which Native American tribes could achieve "tribal economic development, self-sufficiency, and strong tribal governments."

As dependent sovereign nations Indian tribes have a unique relationship with state governments. Activities that are illegal in a state cannot be legal on a reservation located in that state (this is the operational meaning of "dependent"). Tribes cannot be prohibited from engaging in activities that are legal in the state in which they are located (because of their "sovereignty"). When a state legalizes lotteries, bingo, and charity games, Indian

HUMOROUSLY REFERRED TO AS "THE STATE BIRD," CONSTRUCTION
CRANES PROCEED WITH WORK ON THE LAS VEGAS HILTON'S STAR TREK
ATTRACTION (TOP). THE MONTE CARLO (BOTTOM) IS A RECENTLY
COMPLETED "STRIP" PROPERTY MARKETED TO "HIGH ROLLERS."

tribes can develop casino gambling. This is why tribes in Utah, for example, do not have gambling. Since no form of gambling is legal in that state, none of the tribes in the state can have gambling enterprises.

Not all tribes have casinos, and not all Native Americans benefit from them. For example, those who have left reservations and/or are not recognized as tribal members do not share in tribal economic benefits from gambling. In addition, there is a good deal of variation in how successful and profitable tribal gambling operations actually are.

Following the passage of IGRA, numerous conflicts developed between tribes and states over the issue of what kinds of gambling were legal. The degree and kind of regulation states could impose on tribal gaming operations was also debated.

To further complicate matters, tribes can operate gambling enterprises on reservations and on off-reservation "tribal trust lands," land that tribes purchase but which is held "in trust" by the Bureau of Indian Affairs (BIA). The BIA has taken the position that it will only approve the establishment of gambling enterprises on tribal trust lands if there is local approval for the gambling project (casino) and if the project is approved by the governor of the state in which the land is located.

In the agreements (called compacts) that states negotiate with tribes, the state plays an "oversight" role. It must approve the gaming equipment vendors, it has the authority to conduct investigations and audits, and it can prosecute criminal violations on tribal lands. The state also enforces public health and safety standards. Tribes usually contribute to the cost of state regulation and enforcement, but states typically receive no revenues from tribal gaming. There are exceptions, which will be discussed in chapter 6.

Although states do not benefit financially from tribal gaming enterprises, a few tribes make voluntary contributions to the state. However, states may gain indirectly from taxes paid by nontribal businesses that benefit from increased tourism stimulated by tribal gambling.

As of the end of February 1997, Native American tribes in twenty-four states had negotiated compacts and were operating a total of 142 casinos (Christiansen, 1997: 55). While the handle for Native American bingo halls has not increased much in recent years, the growth of casino gambling has been substantial—more than 4,754 percent between 1990 and 1996. In 1996, Native American casinos and bingo halls combined accounted for 11.1 percent of the gambling industry's total handle, up 2.2 percent from the year before.

Gross Revenues

Gross gambling revenues can be summarized quickly. Table 4.4 presents data on gross revenues using the same categories shown in table 4.1.

For the gambling industry as a whole, revenues were up 357 percent between 1982 and 1996. Not surprisingly, the pari-mutuel segment lagged behind other segments and revenues from betting at horse and dog tracks decreased. Off-track betting (on both horses and dogs) experienced modest gains, with ITW betting lower but still positive. OTB and ITW rev-

**TABLE 4.4   Gross Annual Revenue, 1982–1996
(billions of dollars)**

	1982	1990	1991	1992	1993	1994	1995	1996	Percentage Change 1982–1996
Pari-Mutuels									
Horses									
Tracks	1.85	2.10	1.98	1.94	1.82	1.16	0.95	0.82	−56
OTB	0.40	0.81	0.86	0.97	1.04	0.91	1.03	1.06	+165
ITW[c]	—	—	—	—	—	0.87	1.08	1.27	+46
Total*	2.25	2.90	2.84	2.91	2.86	2.94	3.07	3.15	+40
Greyhounds									
Tracks	0.43	0.69	0.70	0.68	0.68	0.51	0.44	0.34	−21
OTB[e]	—	a	0.01	0.01	0.02	0.02	0.03	0.02	+100
ITW[c]	—	—	—	—	—	0.10	0.14	0.15	+50
Total*	0.43	0.70	0.71	0.69	0.70	0.63	0.61	0.50	+16
Jai Alai	0.11	0.11	0.10	0.09	0.08	0.07	0.06	0.05	+54
Total Pari-mutuels*	2.79	3.71	3.65	3.69	3.65	3.64	3.75	3.71	+33
Lotteries									
Traditional Games	2.17	10.19	10.10	11.21	12.42	13.66	14.62	15.34	+606
Video Lotteries[d]	—	0.10	0.12	0.24	0.39	0.46	0.62	0.88	+780
Total Lotteries*	2.17	10.29	10.23	11.46	12.82	14.13	15.24	16.22	+647
Casinos									
Nevada/ New Jersey Slots	2.00	4.89	5.24	5.83	6.17	6.60	7.09	7.29	+264

(continued)

49

TABLE 4.4 (continued)

	1982	1990	1991	1992	1993	1994	1995	1996	Percentage Change 1982–1996
Nevada/ New Jersey Tables	2.20	3.41	3.20	3.12	3.23	3.57	3.86	3.78	+72
Cruise Ships[b,d]	—	0.26	0.29	0.30	0.32	0.36	0.41	0.43	+65
Riverboats[e]	—	—	0.08	0.42	1.46	3.26	4.65	5.54	+6,825
Land-based and Other[d]	—	0.16	0.22	0.47	1.37	1.58	2.00	2.10	+1,212
Total Casinos*	4.20	8.73	9.04	10.14	12.54	15.37	18.01	19.14	+356
Bookmaking									
Sports	0.01	0.05	0.05	0.05	0.08	0.12	0.08	0.08	+200
Horse	0.02	0.08	0.06	0.05	0.04	0.09	0.02	0.01	−50
Total Books*	0.03	0.13	0.11	0.10	0.12	0.21	0.10	0.09	+200
Card Rooms	0.05	0.66	0.66	0.66	0.66	0.73	0.76	0.68	+1,260
Charity Bingo	0.78	1.02	1.05	1.09	1.04	1.04	0.98	0.95	+22
Other Charity Games	0.40	1.19	1.23	1.30	1.29	1.36	1.50	1.48	+270
Indian Reservations									
Bingo[d]	—	0.39	0.42	0.43	0.44	0.45	0.48	0.63	+62
Casinos[d]	—	0.10	0.30	1.07	2.16	2.97	3.56	4.73	+4,630
Total Indian Reservations*[d]	—	0.49	0.72	1.50	2.59	3.42	4.04	5.36	+994
Grand Total*	10.41	26.21	26.68	29.93	34.70	39.90	44.39	47.62	+357

Notes
*In some cases figures in columns will not add to the total because of rounding error.
— Indicates data not available or activity did not exist.
a. Less than $0.01 billion.
b. Figures for 1995 and 1996 include "cruises to nowhere."
c. Change from 1994 to 1996.
d. Change from 1990 to 1996.
e. Change from 1991 to 1996.
Sources: E. M. Christiansen et al., "1991 Gross Annual Wager, Part II: Revenue," Gaming and Wagering Business, 13, no. 8 (August 15, 1992–September 14, 1992): 5, 18; E. M. Christiansen and P. A. McQueen, "1992 Gross Annual Wager, Part II: Revenue," Gaming and Wagering Business, 14, no. 8 (August 15, 1993–September 14, 1993): 12; E. M. Christiansen et al., "1993 Gross Annual Wager," Gaming and Wagering Business, 15, no. 8 (August 5, 1994): 20; E. M. Christiansen et al., "1994 Gross Annual Wager," Gaming and Wagering Business, 16, no. 8 (August 1995): 40; E. M. Christiansen et al., "1995 Gross Annual Wager," Gaming and Wagering Business, 17, no. 8 (August 1996): 68; E. M. Christiansen et al., "1996 Gross Annual Wager," Gaming and Wagering Business, 18, no. 8 (August 1997): 24.

enues helped offset the decrease in revenues at horse and dog tracks, but racing still experienced revenue gains well below the gambling industry's overall average.

The substantial growth of lottery sales (handle) is reflected in revenues for this segment of the gambling industry. Revenues for "traditional" lottery games (i.e., drawings for large prizes, scratch-off and pull-tab games) increased at a much higher rate between 1982 and 1996 (602 percent) than did revenues for the entire gambling industry. Even greater were the revenues from video lotteries operated by state lotteries. Although video lotteries are a small part of the national gambling industry, the increase in revenues attests to their popularity and indicates that they are a significant and growing source of income for state lotteries.

Revenues for casino gambling (excluding Native American reservation casinos) increased from 1982 to 1996 at almost exactly the same rate as the overall gambling industry. Nevada/New Jersey slots had a much bigger increase in revenues than did table games in those major casino venues. Slot and video poker machines have become a more important source of revenue for Nevada/New Jersey casinos than table games (blackjack, craps, poker, roulette, and baccarat).

As was the case with handle, riverboat casinos experienced a huge increase in revenues. In fact, they experienced the largest percentage increase in revenues of all the categories of gambling activities identified in table 4.4. If the American gambling industry has had a "hot spot" in recent years, riverboat casinos (followed rather closely by Indian reservation casinos) was clearly it.

Bookmaking's revenues have been flat for horse racing, but sports betting revenues experienced a solid increase, even though they were below the industry average. Although they are a small part of the gambling industry, card rooms increased their revenues about three and one-half times the overall industry average.

Increases in revenues for charity bingo were small between 1982 and 1996. However, the revenues of "other charity games" were more substantial, though they were below the industry average.

Revenues for Native American reservations experienced a huge increase between 1990 and 1996 and exceeded the gambling industry average by nearly thirteen times. Based on increases in handle and revenues, Native American casinos and riverboat casinos are the most rapidly growing segments of the gambling industry.

Revenues as a Percent of Handle

How do different segments of the gambling industry vary in their ability to retain (i.e., take from players) the money that is gambled? Table 4.5 presents 1996 revenues as a percent of handle. These figures cannot be equated with the "profitability" of different kinds of gambling since they do not take into account total operating expenses (e.g., salaries, taxes, interest on loans, the cost of new construction, replacement of equipment, etc.). They simply tell us what proportion of handle is retained by the gambling operation or activity (revenues). This is essentially the "hold percentage" for the game or location.

TABLE 4.5   Revenue as a Percent of Handle, 1996

Pari-Mutuels		Casinos	
Horses		Nev./N.J. Slots	5.7
Tracks	20.5	Nev./N.J. Tables	2.1
OTB	22.1	Cruise Ships	7.0
ITW	21.2	Riverboats	5.2
Total	21.0	Land-based and Other	9.3
Greyhounds		Total Casinos	4.4
Tracks	22.7	Bookmaking	
OTB	*	Sports	3.2
ITW	21.4	Horse	*
Total	21.7	Total Books	3.5
Jai Alai	25.0	Card Rooms	6.9
Total Pari-mutuels	21.2	Charity Bingo	23.8
Lotteries		Other Charity Games	26.0
Traditional Games	45.2	Indian Reservations	
Video Lotteries	9.8	Bingo	30.0
Total Lotteries	37.8	Casinos	8.0
		Total Indian Reservations	8.2
		Grand Total	8.1

*Handle and/or revenues are too small to provide a reliable calculation.
Source: Calculated from data in tables 4.1 (Handle) and 4.4 (Revenue).

There is a great deal of variation in the hold percentage of different gambling activities. Traditional lottery games (i.e., drawings for large prizes) operated by state governments have the highest hold percentage by a considerable margin (45.2 percent). Lotteries offer gamblers the poorest chance of getting back their bets because only 54.8 percent (100 minus 45.2) is returned to the players in the form of prizes.

Bingo games (charity bingo and games played at Indian reservation bingo halls) and other charity games ("casino nights," "Las Vegas Nights") have the next highest hold percentage. Here the hold ranges between 23.8 percent for charity bingo and 30.0 percent for Indian reservation bingo.

Despite the fact that horse and dog racing have been lagging behind the rest of the gambling industry in terms of both handle and revenues, racing has a comparatively high hold percentage. Horse and dog racing have similar hold percentages ranging from 21.0 to 21.7 percent.

It is difficult to compare different parts of the casino industry. For example, cruise ships and Indian reservation casinos include slots and table games, but the data available for Nevada and New Jersey present information on these games separately. In general, hold percentage is related to how closely regulated an activity is and how much competition it faces. Unregulated cruise ships and Indian reservation casinos (which are less regulated than Nevada and New Jersey casinos) have higher hold percentages. Their relatively isolated locations also mean that they have a more "captive audience" compared to Nevada and New Jersey casinos, where people can walk next door or across the street to a competitor. Consequently, cruise ships and remote casinos can set their machine game payoffs lower and establish table game rules that reduce players' chances of winning, thereby maximizing their hold.

Nevada and New Jersey casino table games and slots have the lowest hold percentage. These casinos face the stiffest competition and are the most closely regulated. The hold percentage for Nevada sports books is also comparatively low.

Summary

Casino gambling (on and off Indian reservations and on riverboats) has experienced the most explosive growth. Lottery growth has been steady and substantial, but the racing segment of the industry has not kept pace.

Riverboat and Indian reservation casinos have grown at a higher rate than those in Nevada and New Jersey. And in Nevada and New Jersey, mechanical games (slots and video poker) have grown substantially in relative importance compared to table games.

The "hold percentage" varies greatly between different segments of the gambling industry. It is highest for lotteries, followed by bingo (both charity and noncharity) and racing. Slot machines in Nevada and New Jersey have the lowest hold percentage. The amount of handle retained by gambling operators is affected by the regulation and competitiveness of the environment in which the games occur.

Chapter 5

Economic Impacts of the Gambling Industry

Gambling is big business and an important industry from an economic point of view. What kind of economic impact does the gambling industry have? This question has been raised in recent years as new jurisdictions (in contrast to the established jurisdictions of Nevada and Atlantic City) consider legalizing new forms of gambling or expanding existing ones. In August 1996 federal legislation created the National Gambling Impact Study Commission to examine the social and economic impacts of gambling in the United States.

One of the main difficulties in addressing the issue of gambling's economic impacts is the dearth of truly objective, unbiased research. Research that looks in a balanced way at both the positive and negative impacts is in short supply. Proponents of new gambling projects (those likely to own and/or operate them) typically overstate the employment opportunities they are likely to create and the tax revenues they might generate. Critics of gambling and those who oppose it for a variety of reasons tend to focus on the economic and social costs associated with gambling and play down its positive aspects. This chapter summarizes both the positive and negative economic impacts of gambling.

Positive Impacts

Casinos

One of the best sources of information on the positive impacts of casino gambling epitomizes the dilemma referred to earlier. In December 1996, Arthur Andersen, a highly respected economic research firm, published the results of its study, *Economic Impacts of Casino Gaming in the United States* (Andersen 1996). The study was prepared for (i.e., paid for) by the American Gaming Association, an organization whose main purpose is to represent, protect, and advocate the economic and political interests of the U.S. casino industry. While the report presents a wealth of reliable data about the economic benefits of casino gambling, it consciously and explicitly ignores its economic or social costs, such as law enforcement, infrastructure construction and maintenance, and compulsive gambling.

The Andersen study deals with all gambling activities that occur within land-based, dockside, and riverboat casinos. It does not deal with Native American reservation or cruise ship casinos. Unless otherwise indicated, the data presented in the summary that follows are for 1995.

According to the study, the casino industry is a significant source of direct employment, employing approximately 284,000 people who are paid $7.3 billion annually. When tips and benefits are included, casino employees' average wage is $26,000, virtually identical to the national average for 1995.

The study also estimates that an additional 400,000 jobs representing $10 billion in wages are indirectly "supported" by the casino industry. These jobs include supplying goods and services, construction and maintenance of casinos, and supplying equipment, food, accounting services, computers, and financial services.

It is undeniable that the gambling industry, casinos in particular, creates employment opportunities. But how do casino employees view their jobs? One study, sponsored by the American Gaming Association and carried out by Coopers and Lybrand (1997), attempted to address this issue. This study concluded that casino employees have benefitted from increased job stability, increased purchasing power, improved health care benefits, and educational and training opportunities. Only 14 percent of the 178,000 questionnaires distributed to employees of one hundred casinos were returned. This extremely low response rate makes the findings highly questionable. In another study done in 1996, Harrah's surveyed 22,000 of its employees in the twelve communities in which it operates casinos. A majority reported that casino employment had led to improved health care, improved education and job skills, and greater financial stability. Twelve percent reported that their casino jobs made it possible for them to get off welfare, and 19 percent indicated that because of their casino employment they were able to stop collecting unemployment compensation benefits (Harrah's, 1997).

Another perspective on casino employees is provided in a study by Yvonne Stedham and Merwin Mitchell (1996). They note that voluntary turnover in the hotel-gaming industry is extremely high. In 1993, the annual turnover rate was 60.3 percent, compared to 6.4 percent in manufacturing industries and 10.4 percent in nonmanufacturing industries. Stedham and Mitchell surveyed employees of six large Reno, Nevada, casinos. Their survey had a 45.5 percent response rate and resulted in usable responses from a little over five hundred nonsupervisory employees. About one-quarter of the respondents were dealers and another one-quarter held jobs on the casino floor (cashier, change, Keno, slots). The remainder held a variety of jobs, including bartender, waiter, cocktail waitress, cook and other kitchen jobs, custodian, maid, maintenance worker, porter, desk clerk, bellhop, security, and valet parking.

Employees of these six casinos appear to be less transient than the high turnover rate for the hotel-gaming industry would lead one to expect. On average, they had been with their current employer nearly three years, had lived in the Reno area for eleven years, and had worked for 1.7 casinos during the previous five years (Stedham and Mitchell, 1996: 279). On a scale with a minimum score of 1 and a maximum score of 5, these casino employees generally responded with "average" ratings (scores between 2.8 and 3.7) for such things as control over how many hours they worked and when they worked, whether their supervisor followed the rules, whether decisions were made in an arbitrary manner, and whether their employer was concerned with their well-being. Employees' satisfaction with supervisors and co-workers and with employee benefits tended to be "polarized." Sizeable numbers of employees gave very positive responses and comparable numbers responded quite negatively (p. 280).

The existence of casinos creates demand for the goods and services of nongambling businesses. *Gaming and Wagering Business* magazine publishes an annual directory of more than one thousand businesses serving the casino, lottery, and pari-mutuel segments of the gambling industry. Many of the businesses are unique to the gambling industry (for example, slot/video machine manufacturing, sales, and service; instant lottery ticket production) but many businesses that operate in a nongambling context have branched out to serve this growing industry (companies that provide interior design, funds transfer systems, signage, furniture, security, and advertising).

The casino industry experienced considerable growth and expansion during the 1990s. That expansion was financed by a large investment of money. The Andersen study estimates that $12.8 billion was spent on new construction, expansion, remodeling, and refurbishment of casinos between 1993 and 1995. Clearly, expenditures of this magnitude have reverberating effects throughout the economy.

In addition, local and state governments and the federal government receive approximately $2.9 billion in taxes from the total revenues of casinos. That figure includes income, sales, and property taxes, but most of it (65 percent) is taxes paid on revenues from gambling, which vary from state to state and range from 3 to 20 percent.

An analysis of the economic impact of gambling has been done by Michael Evans, an economist at Northwestern University (Evans Group,

1996). The Evans study was commissioned by International Game Technology, a major manufacturer of slot, videopoker, and other gambling machines. Like the Andersen study, it focused almost exclusively on the positive economic impacts of gambling.

Evans concluded that throughout the United States the recent establishment of casinos has resulted in a rise in employment and a decrease in unemployment. This study also stresses that tax revenues have increased as a result of legalized casino gambling. Evans estimated that even if the number of casinos remains constant, total direct tax revenues received by state and local governments from casino gambling will rise to $5.3 billion by 2005 (Evans Group, 1996: 1–3).

Lotteries

Lotteries operated by state governments are another segment of the gambling industry with significant economic impacts. National data on the number of people directly employed in the operation of lotteries are not available. The Wisconsin Gaming Commission, responsible for regulating racing and charitable bingo and the state lottery, had 212.65 employees in 1995. If we assume that Wisconsin is somewhat average (and it is in terms of lottery sales), the nation's thirty-six lotteries provide direct employment for an estimated 7,632 people (Wisconsin Legislative Reference Bureau, 1995). No estimates are available for the number of jobs indirectly created by lotteries in such supplier industries as the printing of tickets and cards and the manufacture of computer technology.

In 1996, state lotteries across the country had total sales (i.e., handle) of $36.6 billion. On average, state lotteries retain 56.9 percent of all lottery sales. After deducting operating expenses and the prizes paid out from total sales, a total of $11.6 billion was earned by state governments (McQueen, 1997). While there is variation from state to state, these revenues are added to general revenues or, more typically, specified for particular purposes such as education, programs for the elderly, parks and recreation, property tax relief, economic development, and a variety of public works.

Some Indirect Impacts

A specialized industry has developed to provide information, advice, and a "helping hand" to avid gamblers. Books and computer software programs designed to give gamblers an edge can be described as "how to" publications: how to play different games, wager, handicap, and so on. Gambler's Book Shop in Las Vegas has one of the most complete inventories of these publications and software programs. Its catalog offers over sixty software programs and four hundred and fifty books with such titles as *The Theory of Blackjack, Win at Video Poker, Break the One-Armed Bandits, Beat the Craps out of the Casinos, Horses Talk—It Pays to Listen,* and *Play Poker, Quit Work and Sleep to Noon.* It is impossible to say with any precision how many jobs exist because of these publications and programs or how much tax revenues they generate; they represent an interesting spin-off from the growth of interest and participation in gambling.

Local Community Impacts

The Arthur Andersen study looked at the impact of riverboat casinos in three communities—Shreveport/Bossier City, Louisiana (four casinos); Biloxi/Gulfport, Mississippi (ten casinos); and Joliet, Illinois (two casinos) (Andersen, 1997).

The motivation for developing riverboat casinos has been the belief that they will "revitalize" local communities by providing employment opportunities that benefit individuals and tax revenues that benefit local governments. The Andersen study found that all three communities experienced substantial job growth with the opening of the casinos. Between 1993 and 1994, over half of the 10,000 new jobs created in Shreveport/Bossier City were attributable to the casinos. More than 60 percent of the 18,100 new jobs created in Biloxi/Gulfport since 1990 were a result of the casinos. In Joliet, however, only 25 percent of the new jobs created between 1990 and 1995 were due to the opening of the casinos.

In addition to creating jobs, the wages paid to casino employees are significant. In 1995, the wages paid were: Shreveport/Bossier City, $115 million; Biloxi/Gulfport, $240 million; and Joliet, $103 million. Average casino employee earnings in 1995 ranged from $22,000 in Biloxi/Gulfport to $26,000 in Joliet, with Shreveport/Bossier City averaging $22,500. In Biloxi/Gulfport, in 1995, casino jobs accounted for 13 percent of the area's total employment.

Casino gambling is an important source of tax revenues in all three of these communities. In 1996, the total state and local taxes paid by casinos on gambling revenues was: Shreveport/Bossier City, $110 million; Biloxi/Gulfport, $76 million; and Joliet, $82 million. In 1995, 20 percent of Biloxi's total tax revenues came from casinos.

The Evans study discussed earlier also addresses the economic impact of casino (and other) gambling on particular communities and jurisdictions. For example, Evans points out that since the mid-1970s the economy of Nevada has had an average annual growth rate of 4.6 percent compared to 2.8 percent for the United States as a whole, due in large part to the expansion of casino gambling (Evans Group, 1996: i).

Evans concludes that, in Atlantic City and the county in which it is located, casinos have created 103,000 jobs through direct and indirect employment. He expects them to add an additional 80,000 jobs by 2005. Casino revenues and the state lottery accounted for 8.1 percent of the taxes collected by the state of New Jersey in 1995 and that figure is expected to increase to 12.1 percent by 2005 (Evans Group, 1996: i).

Tunica, Mississippi, provides one of the more dramatic examples of how riverboat casino gambling can improve employment opportunities and enhance tax revenues. It is frequently used as an example of how casino gambling can be a positive force in community economic development. In the late 1980s, the Reverend Jesse Jackson referred to Tunica County in northwest Mississippi as "America's Ethiopia" because of its status as the nation's poorest county. In the early 1990s, unemployment stood at 17 percent. Riverboat casinos arrived in 1992, and their growth has been spectacular. While the number has varied, ten were operating in 1996. By 1994, unemployment had dropped to around 3 percent (Plume, 1994; Smith, 1994).

A few studies have been done on the economic impacts of Native American reservation casinos. Generally, they conclude that the impacts on the reservations, the economy of immediate local areas, and the economy of the states in which they are located have been positive. For example, in Wisconsin, over half of the casino employees were Native Americans, casino employment opportunities reduced unemployment by 1,400, and 820 people were able to get off welfare because of casino employment (Murray, 1993). In Michigan, over half of casino employees were tribal members (University Associates, 1992). In Minnesota, an estimated 20 percent increase in employment was attributed to casino jobs (Midwest Hospitality Advisors, 1992; KPMG Peat Marwick, 1992), but in Arizona a study of one reservation (Fort McDowell located near Phoenix) found that only 5 percent of casino employees were tribal members. The Arizona study found that the Fort McDowell reservation, which has one of the most successful of the state's sixteen tribal casinos, also has unemployment and poverty rates among the lowest of all the reservations in the state (Anders, 1996).

In Colorado, three small former mining towns offer an interesting case study of mixed (positive and negative) economic impacts of casino gambling. Black Hawk, Central City (both located west of Denver), and Cripple Creek (located west of Colorado Springs), began operating casinos in 1991. In an extensive case study of these communities, Patricia Stokowski concluded that the results have been mixed. On the one hand, casinos have been economically rewarding for casino operators and for local, county, and state governments. However, there have been economic, political, environmental, and cultural costs. Traffic volume, crime, and alcohol-related deaths have increased. Many small, locally owned businesses have closed down fol-

RIVERBOAT CASINOS HAVE NOT LIVED UP TO THEIR EXPECTATIONS IN TERMS OF STIMULATING TOURISM AND ECONOMIC DEVELOPMENT. DOWNTOWN ELGIN, ILLINOIS (TOP), HAS SEEN FEW BENEFITS FROM THE GRAND VICTORIA CASINO (BOTTOM) LOCATED ONLY A FEW BLOCKS AWAY.

lowing the opening of externally owned casino development projects. In general, local residents believe that the quality of life in these communities has declined (Stokowski, 1992, 1996).

With fifty-two casinos and an estimated $410 million in annual gambling revenues, these small, rural communities have been transformed into "Disneyesque" tourist destinations that threaten both the historic nature of the communities and their quality of life (O'Driscoll, 1997). As one commentator described the situation, the Colorado towns "have gotten more than they bargained for. Instead of a few slot machines, full-blown casinos owned by Las Vegas veterans and real-estate developers have swept in, swallowing many mom-and-pop businesses along the way. Water, sewer, and traffic systems have been overwhelmed, crime has increased, noncasino businesses face huge tax increases, and the relative calm of local politics has been shattered" (Charlier, 1992).

Negative Impacts

Bankruptcy

About the only national data available on the negative impacts of gambling have to do with gambling and bankruptcy. The SMR Research Corporation, a private economic research organization, conducted a unique study using 1996 bankruptcy filings throughout the United States. Of the more than 3,100 counties in the nation, 298 have at least one major gambling facility (casino, horse or dog racing track, or jai alai fronton). In 1996, the national personal bankruptcy rate per 1,000 population was 4.20. In counties without a major gambling facility, the rate was 3.96. However, in counties with at least one facility, the bankruptcy rate was 4.67—18 percent higher than in those without a facility. In counties with five or more gambling facilities, the rate was 5.33—35 percent higher than in counties without a facility (SMR Research Corporation, 1997).

Several other patterns involving bankruptcy and proximity to gambling facilities emerged in this study. In Nevada, the bankruptcy rate was 50 percent higher than the national average. The counties in which Las Vegas and Reno are located had the highest bankruptcy rates in the state, and the closer a county was to these two major gambling centers, the higher its bankruptcy rate. In New Jersey, the bankruptcy rate in Atlantic County (in which Atlantic City is located) was 7.1, or 71 percent higher than the state average. And with one exception, the closer a county is to Atlantic City, the higher its bankruptcy rate. California presents a similar picture. The counties with the highest bankruptcy rates are Riverside and San Bernardino, which are the counties closest to Las Vegas. Sacramento County has the fourth highest rate, and it is the county closest to Reno. Even though it is comparatively a very small state, Connecticut has two Indian reservation casinos, one of which is the largest in the country. Since 1990, its bankruptcy rate has risen twice as fast as the national rate (SMR Research Corporation, 1997: 117–118).

Perhaps the most interesting case of gambling availability and bankruptcy is Tunica, Mississippi, and the area surrounding it. Recall that Tunica was discussed earlier as an example of the positive economic impact of gambling, with reduction of unemployment, job creation, and increases in local tax revenues resulting from the presence of casino gambling. The highest county bankruptcy rate in the nation is in Shelby County, Tennessee, in which Memphis is located. The rate is 17.28, more than four times the national average. Memphis is only forty miles from Tunica, Mississippi, which has ten waterborne casinos and, along with Gulfport and Biloxi, has seen rapid expansion of casino gambling during the 1990s. Besides Shelby County, counties in the tri-state area surrounding Memphis, in Tennessee, Mississippi, and Arkansas, rank among the nation's highest in terms of bankruptcy rates. In fact, ten of the twenty-four counties with the highest bankruptcy rates in the nation are located in these three states (SMR Research Corporation, 1997: 122).

Besides this information on bankruptcy, there are no other national data on negative impacts that might counterbalance the positive impacts discussed earlier. However, there are a number of state studies, case studies, and "arguments" that identify economic costs that can be considered negative impacts.

Robert Goodman (1995) has argued strongly that many of the economic benefits of legalized gambling are exaggerated and that the negative economic effects are overlooked. For example, he notes that surveys of lottery players in Massachusetts, Kansas, and Wisconsin indicate that lower income people spend a larger proportion of their incomes on lottery tickets compared to those with higher incomes (pp. 39–40). He also cites a survey of 1,000 Atlantic City and Las Vegas casino gamblers that found that lower income people spend a larger proportion of their incomes when they gamble in casinos (p. 42).

Competition

Another negative impact has occurred as a result of competition between different segments of the gambling industry. As casino gambling and lotteries expanded in the late 1980s and early 1990s, the horse racing segment of the industry was adversely affected. As we saw in chapter 4, the racing segment did not keep up with growth in the rest of the gambling industry, and in some places it actually declined.

In several states, legislatures and regulatory commissions bailed the tracks out with subsidies. For example, in New Jersey, the state reduced revenues on pari-mutuel racing to 0.5 percent of the handle by 1998 in an effort to keep tracks viable. After Texas began its lottery in 1992, the handle at the state's racetracks declined by 35 percent. In 1993, Texas lowered its tax rate on the tracks from 6.5 percent to 2 percent. In 1994, Illinois lowered its tax rate on horse racetracks after they were hurt by expanded riverboat casinos and the state lottery. By 1993 one of Wisconsin's five greyhound tracks had gone bankrupt, and only one showed a profit. Another track, located only a few miles from one of the state's larger Native American casinos, closed in 1996. In 1993, taxes on charity gambling were used to subsidize some of the expenses of the tracks (Goodman, 1995: 91–92).

Failed Expectations

Many riverboat casinos were started with the promise and expectation that they would be a stimulus to local tourism and economic development. Certainly in Illinois and Iowa, riverboats were expected to have "spin-off" effects, revitalizing the economies of the communities in which they were located with new (noncasino) jobs and new businesses. By and large, this has not happened. Typically, their customers are locals and "daytrippers," who arrive and depart by automobile or bus and spend little money off the boats. Their expenditures tend to occur on the boats while gambling and at the boats' associated dining facilities and shops. Earl Grinol, an economist at the University of Illinois, concluded that Illinois riverboats have not produced the jobs that they promised and have had little effect on the unemployment rate. His study of ten Illinois counties where riverboats had opened between September 1990 and June 1993 found that casinos directly added 7,806 jobs, total employment rose by only 2,038, and the number of unemployed people decreased by only 21. The implication is that many people left noncasino jobs to take jobs in casinos (Grinol, 1994a, 1994b).

There is additional evidence that riverboat casinos do not generate tourism. In 1995 Thompson and Gazel (1996) interviewed 785 gamblers at five Illinois riverboat casinos (Joliet, Elgin, Alton, Aurora, and Rock Island). They found that 61 percent were local residents (defined as people living within thirty-five miles of the casinos). Nonlocal Illinois residents made up an additional 22 percent of the gamblers, and 17 percent were from other states. Overnight stays in the towns were rare; 98 percent of those interviewed stayed less than a day, and only 3 percent spent money off the riverboat.

Atlantic City has had similar experiences. Despite the popularity of its casinos, there have been few economic benefits to the broader community. Day-trippers from New York and Philadelphia confine their activities and spending to the casinos and the food and shopping services they provide. Atlantic City has not become a tourism destination resort leading to broad-based economic growth and development.

With some notable exceptions, the same situation holds for Indian reservation casinos. They, too, draw on a local clientele and day-trippers. For example, a 1994 Wisconsin study of reservation casino patrons found that 80 percent were from Wisconsin (15 percent were from the four adjacent states of Michigan, Illinois, Iowa, and Minnesota). Of the Wisconsin residents, 62 percent could be described as "locals," living within fifty miles of the casino they visited. Only 18 percent lived more than one hundred miles away. Of the 697 casino visitors interviewed, 74 percent said that they were staying in the immediate area of the casino less than one day (Thompson et al., 1995). An exception to this general pattern is the Mashantucket Pequot's Foxwoods casino in Ledyard, Connecticut, which has developed into a destination resort.

Summary

Balanced, unbiased assessments of the positive and negative impacts of gambling are hard to come by. It is clear that, on the national level, the gambling industry is a major employer and that taxes on gambling revenues are significant. Indirectly, the gambling industry is also an important consumer of the services of numerous other industries and of the members of particular occupations.

At the local community level, casinos in particular have created jobs and revenues from riverboat operations and on Native American reservations. Outside Nevada and Atlantic City, the ability of casinos to increase tourism has been limited at best and disappointing at worst. Riverboat casinos tend to attract day-trippers, while Native American reservations tend to attract day-trippers and "locals." In Colorado, casinos have led to economic growth but, in the view of many local residents, at the cost of deterioration in the "quality of life."

Negative economic impacts are less well documented than positive impacts. A national study has demonstrated that proximity to casinos and racetracks is related to high personal bankruptcy rates. At the state level, lottery play appears to be "regressive" in the sense that lower income people spend a larger proportion of their incomes on the lottery. Competition within the gambling industry has produced situations where legislatures and gaming commissions have provided financial subsidies and bailouts, especially to race tracks, thereby reducing the total revenue benefits to states.

65

Chapter 6

Gambling and Public Policy

The term "public policy" has several related meanings. In the broadest sense, public policy refers to whatever governments choose to do or not to do. It can also be thought of as legislative requirements and general principles that guide the actions of public officials. Implicit in the concept of public policy is the idea that those actions protect and promote the public's welfare.

Ideally, public policy is guided by the principle of impartiality, where no group's interests are promoted over those of other groups. But the making of public policy is anything but a benign, rational process guided by the goal of achieving the public good. Special interests, economic issues, and political considerations become elaborately involved in the process. Some special interest groups are more successful than others in getting the attention of legislators, because they have greater financial resources or political "clout." In the case of gambling, the formulation of public policy has been complicated by the fact that government itself has become one of the groups with an economic interest in gambling (especially by virtue of operating lotteries). Government discovered gambling as a source of public revenue and developed an interest in promoting it. Consequently, government cannot impartially assess the claims of other groups regarding the desirability of expanding or contracting legal gambling.

In chapter 3 we noted the recurring ambivalence of Americans toward gambling. That ambivalence is reflected in public policy. Historically, government has been somewhat paternalistic, concerned that gambling would do damage to the poor and disenfranchised (Eadington, 1995). Hence, the longstanding federal policy prohibiting a national lottery. At the same time, governments have used gambling to raise money for public projects (from building ports to arming the Continental Army in the Colonial era) and to raise public revenues for all kinds of purposes in state-run lotteries since the early 1960s.

How Public Policy on Gambling Is Made

Public policy on gambling has been created from a number of sources. These include legislative actions, court rulings, administrative decisions of government agencies, and referenda and initiatives (Rose, 1995).

Legislative Action

Legislative action refers to passing legislation to create state lotteries and authorize state agencies to license dog and horse racetracks, operators of charitable bingo games, and casinos. In some cases, it includes passing legislation to *prohibit* various kinds of gambling.

Legislative procedures differ from state to state. Often, approval by the electorate at a referendum is necessary before the law can be finalized. In 1988, for example, the Wisconsin electorate had to approve a referendum before the bill to create a lottery and legalize pari-mutuel betting on dog, horse, and snowmobile races could become law. In 1993, Wisconsinites had to approve a referendum before the bill prohibiting additional gambling could be law. In both cases, the legislative action and the referenda resulted in amendments to the state's constitution.

Court Rulings

Court rulings are another source of public policy. In recent years, court rulings have been particularly important regarding the kind of gambling that can take place on Indian reservation lands. For example, in 1987 the U.S. Supreme Court ruled in *California v. Cabazon Band of Mission Indians* that a tribe could offer any form of gambling legalized by the state in which the reservation was located, and that the tribe, not the state, had the power to regulate that gambling. The federal 1988 Indian Gaming Regulatory Act established mandatory regulatory systems (Rose, 1995).

Administrative Decisions

Decisions by agencies such as lottery boards and gaming commissions are another source of public policy. For example, lottery boards have decided to add keno games (in California) and video lottery terminals (in West Virginia). The Wisconsin Gaming Commission decided to allow inter-track wagering at dog tracks. This, in effect, created off-track betting and eliminated the need for explicit legislative action or a referendum.

Referenda and Initiatives

Final sources of public policy on gambling are referenda and initiatives. There are many cases of the electorate voting on both binding and advisory proposals that lead to legalization and creation of gambling enterprises or that prohibit their establishment. Examples include the creation of casino gambling in three mountain towns in Colorado and in Deadwood, South Dakota, and riverboat casinos in Iowa and Missouri. In November 1996, voters in Detroit, Michigan, authorized the state gaming commission to issue licenses for up to three casinos in that city. However, voters in eight states turned down a variety of proposals to create new gambling enterprises and expand existing ones, including a proposal to legalize riverboat casinos in Ohio (Doocey, 1996).

A Case Study in Policy Making: Gambling in Wisconsin

The complexities involved in public policy making on gambling are difficult to see if we limit ourselves to broad generalizations. Multiple actors, organizations with a variety of agendas and economic and political interests interact to produce policy outcomes. Because states are the key units involved in setting policies that expand or limit gambling, the following section presents a case study of one state over a limited period of time to illustrate the process.

During a period of approximately six years (1987–1993), Wisconsin went from the legalization of a lottery and pari-mutuel wagering to a constitutional ban on all additional forms of gambling. Since 1993, gambling, nevertheless, has expanded modestly, and proposals to expand and limit gambling continue to be made and debated.

From 1987 to 1993, a number of proposals and arguments were made that could have substantially increased the amount and variety of legal gambling in the state. Examining some of these proposals, and the economic and political factors that eventually determined their fate, illustrates the nonrational and haphazard nature of policy making on gambling.

Wisconsin's experience with legal gambling is very recent. A brief historical summary of key legislation will help put recent policy issues in perspective.

The Legislative and Public Policy Background

When Wisconsin became a state in 1848, antilottery sentiment was quite strong (Clotfelter and Cook, 1989; Findlay, 1986). Like many other states that joined the Union at this time, Wisconsin, through its constitution, explicitly prohibited lotteries and all games of chance. This prohibition remained in place until 1965. In that year, one year after New Hampshire started its landmark lottery, Wisconsin voters approved a constitutional amendment that allowed Wisconsin residents to participate in a variety of sweepstakes, promotions, and contests, both local and national in scope. In 1973 (by which time eight states were operating lotteries) the Wisconsin constitution was amended by referendum to permit the legislature to authorize the licensing of bingo games by religious, charitable, fraternal, service, and veterans organizations. In 1977, the constitution was further amended to permit the legislature to authorize the licensing of raffles by the same types of organizations.

By 1987, twenty-two states and the District of Columbia were operating lotteries, and Wisconsin's constitution was amended again to permit the legislature to authorize a state-operated lottery and pari-mutuel wagering on dog, horse, and snowmobile races. The argument for the lottery was basically the same as it had been in other states: to increase revenues and forestall tax increases. In addition, it was clear that the Illinois lottery and horse race tracks in the Chicago metropolitan area were popular with Wisconsin residents, especially those living in the heavily populated southeastern part of the state. The perception that gambling dollars were being lost to Illinois created a climate favorable to legalization of a lottery. The vote on the amendment was 65 percent for and 35 percent against. The lottery began operation in September 1988.

In 1990 the state attorney general issued an "interpretation" of the 1987 amendment in which the term "lottery" was broadly construed to include any game involving "prize, chance, and consideration." This interpretation was later upheld in a federal court. The interpretation and the court ruling allowed the legislature to authorize state licensing of conventional casino games. Organizations that qualified to operate charitable bingo games and raffles were licensed to operate "Las Vegas Nights" and "Casino Nights." This interpretation and court ruling also set the stage for the mandatory negotiation of compacts with Indian tribes. In 1991 and 1992, gaming compacts were negotiated with all eleven of Wisconsin's Indian tribes under the provisions of the federal 1988 Indian Gaming Regulatory Act.

In April 1993, voters approved an amendment to the constitution to clarify the meaning of the 1987 amendment authorizing the lottery. The 1993 amendment stated that "all forms of gambling are prohibited except bingo,

raffles, pari-mutuel on-track betting and the current state-run lottery and . . .
the state will not conduct prohibited forms of gambling as part of the state-
run lottery." This, in effect, prohibited all forms of casino gambling.

The Scope of Gambling in Wisconsin

Clearly, Wisconsin was a latecomer to legal gambling. After the legalization of the lottery and pari-mutuel wagering, the broad interpretation of
the term *lottery* created a window of opportunity for the establishment of
casinos by Indian tribes. However, in a relatively short period of time
(1987–1993) a substantial gambling industry developed. By the end of 1992,
lottery ticket sales and the handles for greyhound racing, charitable bingo,
and Indian reservation bingo halls and casinos totaled approximately $1.5
billion. Indian gambling enterprises accounted for nearly half (47 percent) of
this total. By 1995, the handle had increased to $7.9 billion, with Indian
reservation casinos accounting for 90 percent of it (Christiansen et al., 1996;
Kenosha News, 1997).

The State Lottery

The state lottery is popular. Sales increased from its introduction in
1988 through 1995, but decreased in 1995 from $511 million to $460 million
in 1996. One survey found that between 55 percent and 61 percent of the
state's residents play the lottery (Piliavin and Rossol, 1995). The lottery operates a variety of games, including on-line games such as Supercash and
Powerball with large prizes as well as instant scratch and pull tab games.
There are a little over five thousand sales outlets, approximately one per
thousand residents.

Charitable Bingo

Charitable bingo games are widely available throughout the state.
They exhibited steady growth from 1975 to 1990. Since then they have declined somewhat in both the handle and the number of licenses issued. This
decline is probably due to the increased availability of Indian operated bingo
games, which offer longer periods of play and larger jackpots, as well as the
recent growth of other forms of gambling (dog racing, lottery games, and
Indian casinos with blackjack and slots).

Greyhound Dog Racing

Following passage of the 1987 constitutional amendment authorizing a lottery and pari-mutuel racing, five dog racing tracks opened by the end
of 1990. One closed in 1993 and another in 1995. Dairyland Greyhound Park

NATIVE AMERICAN CASINOS SUCH AS THE HO CHUNK CASINO NEAR BARABOO, WISCONSIN (TOP), HAVE CREATED SERIOUS COMPETITION FOR THE RACING SEGMENT OF THE GAMBLING INDUSTRY SUCH AS DAIRYLAND GREYHOUND PARK NEAR KENOSHA, WISCONSIN (BOTTOM).

is the only track that has done well financially. It is located in the southeastern corner of the state, approximately sixty miles north of downtown Chicago and forty miles south of downtown Milwaukee. Easily accessible from these two population centers via a major interstate highway, Dairyland draws about one-third of its customers from Illinois.

Geneva Lakes Kennel Club has never been profitable and has lost money since 1994. It, too, is located in the southeastern part of the state, approximately fifty miles west of Dairyland near Lake Geneva, a resort community popular with Illinois as well as Wisconsin residents. While it is easily accessible from Chicago and Milwaukee, it is not as close to these cities (and especially the north Chicago suburbs) as is Dairyland. Both Dairyland and Geneva Lakes experience competition in the form of off-track betting facilities and riverboat casinos in northern Illinois, which are easily accessible to residents of southern Wisconsin.

Wisconsin's three other tracks have consistently lost money. Wisconsin Dells Greyhound Park, which closed in 1995, was located in the popular Wisconsin Dells recreational area north of Madison. However, it could not compete with the Ho Chunk reservation casino located only a few miles away. Fox Valley Greyhound Park closed in 1993. It was located in a region of the state that includes several population centers—Green Bay, Oshkosh, and Appleton. However, it could not compete with the state's largest Indian casino, the Oneida Bingo and Casino, which is located in Green Bay's metropolitan area. St. Croix Meadows Greyhound Racing, located in the far west central part of the state, is within an easy half-hour drive of the Minneapolis/St. Paul metropolitan area. It competes with nearby Wisconsin and Minnesota Indian casinos.

Indian Casinos and Bingo Halls

All eleven of Wisconsin's Indian tribes have negotiated compacts with the state. During the time period 1987 to 1993, they were operating fifteen casinos/bingo halls located mainly in the relatively sparsely populated northern half of the state. However, a high-stakes bingo hall with two hundred slot machines is located near downtown Milwaukee. The casinos have a combined total of 6,000 to 7,000 slot/video poker machines and 250 to 350 blackjack tables. Low-cost one-day and overnight tour bus trips to the casinos are extensively marketed in Milwaukee, Racine, and Kenosha in the southeastern part of the state.

Public Policy Issues

With the introduction of the lottery and dog racing, the major policy issue has been the legalization of additional forms of gambling. Because the state receives revenues from the lottery and dog tracks, enhancing their profitability has also been a concern. The impact of Indian casinos on dog tracks and, to a lesser extent, the lottery has also been an issue.

Public policy on gambling has been shaped by the governor, the legislature, the Gaming Commission, the dog track owners and operators, the Wisconsin Tavern League, the state's tourism industry, economic development groups, local political officials in communities with dog tracks and those wanting gambling enterprises, Indian tribes, and (in a very limited way) the Wisconsin Conference of Churches. Debates about the expansion of gambling have also been shaped by the growth of gambling and proposals for expanding gambling in adjacent states, especially Minnesota, Illinois, and Iowa.

The governor and legislature have not taken a strong, consistent stand on the legalization of gambling in the state. While the governor has been cool to the idea of expanded gambling, he has not been vehemently or consistently opposed to it. In contrast, some legislators have opposed gambling on moral grounds. Others view it as an economic development strategy and favor it as a means of increasing state tax revenues. Legislators from communities with dog tracks have opposed expansion in or near their communities because this would threaten their tracks and the economic benefits to their constituents. Officials from communities that do not have gambling businesses favor expansion as a way of benefiting their communities economically and having something positive to point to at reelection time.

The Wisconsin Gaming Commission, created in 1992 by the merger of the bingo, racing, and lottery boards, is responsible for regulation. However, in a policy vacuum, it has not been reluctant to advise the governor and legislature on policy matters. While the commission has regulatory powers, it also operates the state lottery. Hence, it functions with a built-in conflict: it is expected to operate a profitable lottery while regulating itself and its competitors.

Dog track owners and operators, in an attempt to protect their enterprises from competition, have not been advocates of gambling expansion. Owners and operators in the central and northern parts of the state are concerned about competition from Indian casinos. Those in the southern part of the state have been concerned about the growth of riverboat casinos in Iowa, Illinois, and Indiana, and especially about proposals for land- and water-based casinos in Chicago, an important market on which they draw.

The Wisconsin Tavern League represents the business interests of tavern owners and is an influential lobby in the state. Wisconsin has a pervasive tavern culture in both urban and rural areas. In rural taverns, illegal video poker machines are ubiquitous and routinely confiscated by the police (*Milwaukee Journal,* 1993). The league has advocated the legalization of video poker machines for taverns on the grounds that, without them, owners cannot survive the competition from Indian casinos. It has promoted the idea that because of the Indian monopoly on casino gambling, taverns cannot compete on a "level playing field," a slogan that has been picked up by dog track owners.

The state's tourism industry has a mixed set of interests to consider, and has exhibited internal disagreement on the issue of expanding gambling. In the western part of the state, along the Mississippi River, there has been strong local support for riverboat casinos. These have been seen as a potential economic benefit to any community in which they might be based. Riverboat casinos in Iowa and Illinois, recurring proposals to introduce them in Minnesota, and the growth of Indian casinos in Wisconsin and Minnesota have created the perception that western Wisconsin is losing tourism dollars. In the central and northern parts of the state, tourism is promoted on the basis of wholesome outdoor, family recreation (camping, fishing, boating, hiking, as well as theme park attractions). This image is seen by many people as being at odds with the image and reality of gambling. At the same time, restaurants, hotels, motels, and a variety of retail businesses benefit from the additional tourism stimulated by Indian casinos.

Membership and leadership of economic development groups often overlap with those of tourism industry groups. Cities and towns throughout the state are engaged in efforts to attract new businesses and industries. In discussions of development strategies, the desirability of gambling enterprises is considered alongside other businesses. In communities along the Mississippi River, riverboat gambling is as much an economic development issue as it is a tourism issue.

Local political officials are also important actors in public policy formulation. Their stances tend to be guided by reelection concerns. For example, in Kenosha county where Dairyland Greyhound Park (the state's only successful dog track) is located, local officials frequently remind the public of their roles in bringing the track (and its eight hundred jobs) to the community. They tend to oppose the development of gambling enterprises in the area that would threaten the economic well-being of "their" track. Local officials often base their position on the preferences of their constituencies, whose support they will need at election time. Where pro-riverboat sentiments are strong, local officials tend to favor riverboat casinos and see them as potential contributors to local economic growth (for which they may be able to later claim credit). Officials with antigambling constituencies are predictably against gambling expansion, and often claim the moral high ground when opposing gambling.

The Wisconsin Conference of Churches has consistently opposed gambling and its expansion in the state. It opposed the 1987 amendment that made the lottery and pari-mutuel wagering possible. Its opposition was formulated on moral grounds and on the argument that a lottery would act as a regressive tax. The conference favored the 1993 amendment, which prohibited any new forms of gambling. The conference has not maintained a continuous antigambling campaign, however, and its involvement tends to be episodic.

During 1988, 1989, and 1990, the lottery grew, dog tracks were licensed, built, and commenced operation, and compacts with Indian tribes were negotiated. At the same time, Indian casinos were opening in Minnesota, riverboat casinos were being developed in Iowa and Illinois, and legislation for riverboat casinos was being introduced (but not approved) in the Minnesota legislature. Gambling expansion was not a major issue in the state during this period, although the growth of gambling in surrounding states was beginning to be seen as a threat to existing and developing gambling enterprises in Wisconsin.

In 1991, when Wisconsin Indian tribes began operating casinos, tavern owners and the Wisconsin Tavern League intensified lobbying efforts for video poker machines in taverns. Sentiment for riverboat casinos in the western part of the state increased, and dog track owners were becoming concerned about competition from Indian casinos in Wisconsin and Minnesota and riverboats in Illinois and Iowa. By late 1991, it was clear that the 1992 legislative session would have to deal with gambling expansion issues.

The Governor's Task Force

In December 1991, Governor Tommy G. Thompson appointed the Governor's Blue Ribbon Task Force on Gambling, which included a law school dean, a newspaper publisher, a retired minister, the president of a major tourist attraction in central Wisconsin, an official of the Oneida tribe, an official of a tourism development organization, and a physician. The task force issued its report and recommendations a week before the 1993 legislative session was to begin (Governor's Blue Ribbon Task Force on Gambling, 1992).

The task force acknowledged that gambling enterprises in surrounding states threatened tourism and other businesses in Wisconsin and stressed the economic and revenue benefits that gambling would bring the state. It stressed the need for local approval and careful state regulation of any new forms of gambling. The task force recommended the expansion of gambling in two forms: (1) lottery-operated Video Lottery Terminals (VLTs) in taverns, bowling alleys, and dog tracks, and (2) waterborne casinos, including one boat on the Mississippi River, one on Lake Superior, and two on Lake Michigan. Games on these boats would be limited to VLTs, slot machines, and blackjack.

The task force also made recommendations to limit the expansion of gambling. They suggested that no new pari-mutuel facilities be licensed and that existing dog tracks could only have VLTs (if those became legal).

The task force asked Indian tribes to "voluntarily" limit casinos to one per tribe. The task force also recommended that casinos built by the tribes on newly acquired off-reservation land be within a fifty mile radius of their reservation (a recommendation that seems to imply that the voluntary limit suggestion would or could be ignored).

Finally, the task force recommended that a single gambling regulatory agency be created (which the 1992 legislature did) and that funding be provided for public education, research, and treatment of compulsive gambling.

Response to the Task Force Report

The only task force recommendation that the governor responded to favorably—and only in part—was the one regarding VLT operations. He proposed that legislation be introduced to authorize the licensing of VLTs in taverns, but not at dog tracks, as recommended by the task force. This proposal drew strong opposition from antigambling forces, those favoring the waterborne casinos, and the tourism industry in general. The governor then proposed that the licensing of VLTs in taverns be left to local option. This proposal was received with disbelief and opposed even by the Tavern League. Two taverns at one intersection might be in different jurisdictions, one with VLTs and one without. The tavern in the VLT county would do a booming business, while the one in the non-VLT county would soon be out of business.

The 1992 session of the Wisconsin legislature (including two special sessions on gambling) was dominated by gambling issues. Initial response to the task force report was mixed. Some legislators opposed it, some supported it, while others opposed parts or supported only parts of it. Support and opposition seemed to be based on (a) assumptions about constituents' preferences, (b) arguments for and against the recommendations made by those with something to gain or lose economically, and (c) assumptions about how Wisconsin gambling enterprises and the tourism industry would be affected by developments in surrounding states. A consensus could not be reached on a single position on the expansion issue, creating what can only be called "gridlock."

During this legislative session, two proposals that were not addressed by the task force report contributed even more confusion to the debate. The first was a proposal from an Illinois developer to build a harness racing track in Racine County on a site approximately ten miles north of Dairyland. The state Racing Board enthusiastically endorsed the proposal because the track would provide jobs and tax revenues. The Racing Board expressed doubts about its viability and reaffirmed the moratorium on new pari-mutuel licenses it had imposed two years earlier. The second proposal further complicated matters. A bill permitting out-of-state simulcast wagering at dog tracks passed the legislature. Its passage was an effort to kill the harness racing proposal, because the developer of this project had said that he would not attempt to compete with simulcast wagering. Although the governor vetoed the simulcasting bill, its effect was to lessen the enthusiasm of the proposer of the harness racing track. This entire episode also had the effect of putting anti-expansion legislators from Racine County in the awkward position of opposing a project with potential economic benefits to the local area they represented.

Perhaps the most unpredictable factor contributing to confusion about what to do with the gambling issue came from out of state. In the midst of the Wisconsin legislature's unsuccessful efforts to come up with an expansion policy, Chicago Mayor Richard Daley announced his support for a $2 billion proposal for a hotel/casino entertainment theme park in Chicago. The possibility of a casino in Chicago was interpreted as a threat to southeastern Wisconsin's dog tracks and tourism industry in general.

When the 1992 legislative session ended in early April 1992, the only significant action that had been taken on gambling legislation was the passage of a bill folding the lottery, bingo, and racing boards into a single Gaming Commission. It took two special sessions called by the governor and lasting into July to reach a resolution. In calling these special sessions devoted exclusively to the issue of gambling, the governor proposed a constitutional amendment to explicitly limit gambling to conventional lottery games, charitable bingo, and pari-mutuel racing. After three months of proposals and counterproposals, the legislature passed an amendment to this effect. However, for the state constitution to be amended, the amendment had to pass in two consecutive sessions of the legislature and be approved by voters in a general election. Consequently, final resolution was put off until the 1993 legislature met and a general election could be called.

During the special sessions, an event occurred that shifted sentiment against efforts to legislate new forms of gambling. The Winnebago Indian tribe stated its intention to acquire nonreservation land near Madison, get tribal trust status for it, and build a casino. The location of the proposed site is important: it would have been easily accessible via Interstate 94 from Milwaukee and via Interstate 90 from Chicago. It had the potential of drawing on these two major urban markets. At least as important is the fact that these two highways are the main routes to central and northern Wisconsin's tourism and outdoor recreational areas. While approval of the proposal seemed unlikely, the mere possibility of an Indian casino in this strategic location drew strong opposition from the central Wisconsin tourism industry. The Winnebago already were operating three casinos and bingo halls in the central part of the state. Proponents of Mississippi riverboat casinos renewed their arguments. If the Winnebago proposal came about, they said, the state should legalize riverboats to protect tourism in the western part of the state.

Between the end of the prolonged 1992 legislative session and the beginning of the 1993 session (January 1993) several events served to strengthen antiexpansion sentiment and increase the likelihood of a second legislative approval of the antiexpansion amendment.

In October 1992, operators of the St. Croix Meadows dog track asked the Gaming Commission for permission to add casino games so they could compete with nearby Indian casinos. The proposal was rejected by the commission on the grounds that it did not have the authority to approve the request (*Milwaukee Journal* 1992). Following numerous reports about the track's financial difficulties and possibly closing, the St. Croix Chippewa tribe proposed to buy the track, get tribal trust status for it, and add a complete casino. Although he called for a ban on additional gambling during the 1992 special sessions of the legislature, the governor indicated that he would support the proposal only if there was local support for it. In early December, voters in Hudson approved the sale by a very narrow vote (51.2 percent for and 48.8 percent against). With this mild expression of support the governor chose not to approve the sale, the Gaming Commission expressed opposition, and the proposal died.

The Minnesota Indian Gaming Association also expressed opposition to the St. Croix Chippewa proposal. The proposed dog track/casino in Wisconsin would have drawn customers from the Minneapolis/St. Paul area, which Minnesota Indian casinos depend on for their customers. This suggests that economic interests can be more important than common ethnic identity in determining the position taken by Indian tribes on gambling issues.

A proposal from a different tribe served to further strengthen antigambling sentiments in the legislature. In December, the Lac du Flambeau Chippewa, who operate a casino in the northeastern part of the state, proposed to acquire land in Kenosha County, get tribal trust status, and build a casino. The possible locations were all within five miles of the Dairyland dog track. Local officials, the newspaper, and business leaders came out in strong opposition to the proposal and effectively killed it. They were concerned about the ability of the local dog track to survive the competition. The Lac du Flambeau Chippewa then targeted a location ten miles north in Racine County with a similar proposal that met a similar fate.

While the Lac du Flambeau Chippewa were making their in-state proposals, the St. Croix Chippewa were proposing to build a casino on newly acquired land (for which they would seek tribal trust status) in Illinois, in the northwest Chicago suburbs. This proposal was not pursued—there did not appear to be local support for it. At the time, there were numerous proposals for expanding riverboat casinos in and around Chicago's northern suburbs. From the perspective of those north of the Wisconsin-Illinois border, it appeared that ample gambling opportunities were being discussed to the south, and there was no need to expand gambling in Wisconsin.

Let the Voters Decide: The 1993 Amendment

By the time the 1993 legislature was ready to meet, media editorial support for the "no new gambling" amendment was strong. Public sentiment reflected the view that "we have enough—let's limit gambling to the lottery, bingo, and dog tracks." It was also apparent that the legislature was not about to repeat its prolonged 1992 gambling debate.

The 1993 legislature promptly gave its second approval to the amendment and a general election was scheduled for April 6, 1993. However, the legislature retained five nonbinding referendum questions that it had agreed to seek voter opinion on during the 1992 legislative session.

The two months preceding the April 6 election was a period of extensive media campaigning for and against the amendment. The Wisconsin Indian Gaming Association (WIGA) opposed the amendment, concerned that its passage would make it difficult if not impossible to renew tribal compacts in 1998 and 1999. WIGA's television and newspaper ads stressed the economic benefits of gambling enterprises to the tribes, as well as the spin-off benefits to the non-Indian communities in which they are located. Ads suggested that passage of the amendment would result in closing the casinos. WIGA proposed that the legislature delay a vote on the amendment so that a "mega casino" could be built in the densely populated southeastern part of the state. This, argued WIGA, would allow them to contribute $250 million per year to the state for property tax relief. The proposal appealed to legislators who were concerned about rising property taxes, but support was minimal.

The Wisconsin Conference of Churches and the Roman Catholic Bishops of Wisconsin strongly supported the amendment on moral grounds. While the Bishops affirmed a neutral stand on the morality of gambling per se, they noted that recent trends (presumably the opening of Indian casinos) had moved the state beyond "the point of moderation" (*Racine Journal Times,* 1993a). The Wisconsin Conference of Churches favored the amendment on moral grounds. The chair of the Conference's Gambling Issues Task Force stated that gambling "preys on people's weaknesses and it exploits their foolishness" (*Racine Journal Times,* 1993b).

The governor initially took a neutral position on the amendment. But as the April election approached, he came out in favor of it. By favoring the amendment, the governor risked angering tavern owners and advocates of expanding gambling within the tourism industry (especially proponents of Mississippi riverboat gambling).

Legislators continued to espouse a mixture of positions on the amendment that were generally consistent with their earlier views. Among those advocating passage of the amendment, the most commonly heard argument was that, by limiting gambling to what currently exists, passage of the amendment would protect the viability of the lottery and the dog tracks.

The amendment passed by a state-wide vote of 59 percent. This put to rest the expansion issue, but only temporarily. Proposals from Indian tribes and dog tracks to add casinos to tracks continued to be put forth. The Potawatomi tribe, which owns a bingo hall with two hundred slots near downtown Milwaukee, has proposed construction of a full casino with a hotel, convention facilities, and a shopping mall. The tribe suggested that it would be willing to share revenues with the city. Other tribes have put forward proposals to purchase the dog racing tracks in Hudson and Kenosha. Finally, the opening of riverboat casinos in Indiana on Lake Michigan created new interest in the development of riverboat casinos in Chicago, a development that would create additional competition for Wisconsin gambling interests. The expansion of gambling promises to be an ongoing saga.

Conclusions

What conclusions can be drawn from this case study? First, a complex combination of special interest and lobbying groups shape the policy-making process. Elected officials take positions on gambling with an eye to the interests and response of local constituents and to support for reelection. In other words, gambling policy is shaped by some of the same political forces that bear on other policy issues.

Second, the absence of consensus among public officials (created in part by conflicting interests) can lead to legislative abandonment of responsibility for policy making. In the Wisconsin case, turning the issue over to the electorate to settle through a constitutional amendment resulted from a failure to develop legislative consensus.

Third, existing gambling enterprises that serve as a source of state revenue come to be seen as an investment to be protected when new forms of gambling are considered. In the Wisconsin case, the future of the lottery and dog tracks became a major consideration. A similar situation exists in Illinois, where horse race tracks in the Chicago area have successfully stalled the development of nearby water- and land-based casinos.

Fourth, policy making on gambling within a state is indirectly shaped by developments beyond its borders. While Wisconsin legislators and gambling enterprise operators have no control over what happens in surrounding states, those developments affect the debates about gambling within the state.

Finally, in Wisconsin at least, gambling policy has been affected by hostility toward Indians. It is difficult to document how important a factor this was in the passage of the 1993 constitutional amendment. Negative feelings toward Indians are not difficult to find. Their right to operate casinos when non-Indians could not has been widely seen as "unfair." The perception that a vote *for* the amendment would close down existing casinos or make it more difficult to renew existing compacts provided an opportunity for people with anti-Indian prejudices to express them in a socially acceptable way at the ballot box. Thus, a factor having nothing to do with gambling per se played a role in shaping gambling policy.

The Rationale for Legalization: Jobs, Economic Growth, and Tax Revenues

Legislators' and other public officials' motivation for legalizing and expanding gambling has been similar throughout the United States: creation of jobs, general economic development, and increased tax revenues. It is clear, however, that state governments have embraced lotteries with more enthusiasm than they have casino gambling.

Dombrink and Thompson (1990) examined "campaigns" to legalize casinos in twenty states between 1960 and 1988. While this was a period in which the legalization of lotteries was extensive, only one campaign to legalize casinos, New Jersey in 1976, was successful. Some of these proposals and campaigns to legalize casinos were decided by referenda, while others were settled by legislative action.

Dombrink and Thompson concluded that campaigns to legalize lotteries fit a "gravity model," in which a "preponderance of evidence" favoring legalization results in successful campaigns. However, because of casino gambling's negative images, casino legalization faces a stricter test. Using the parlance of criminal law, they argued that the evidence favoring casino legalization must be conclusive "beyond any reasonable doubt." Dombrink and Thompson refer to this as the "veto model."

According to Dombrink and Thompson, the veto model has four main components, *all* of which must be present for a casino legalization campaign to be successful. The first is the "political environment." This includes the economic conditions of the proposed area for casino development and the state's prior experience with legalized gambling (lottery, racing, and so on).

A weak or depressed economy and positive experiences with already existing gambling favor a successful casino campaign. Second, the active support of political and business elites is important. Active support of the governors, state attorneys general, influential legislators, judges, and business leaders favors casino legalization. Active opposition by other gambling interests such as racetrack owners, charity bingo operators, or lottery officials can undermine casino legalization campaigns. The third component is the credibility and financial resources of those sponsoring the casino legalization campaign. Sponsors must appear to be operating honestly and fairly, and have significant amounts of money to spend to promote casino legalization (and to outspend opponents). The fourth is "campaign issue dominance." Campaigns that take the high ground and focus on economic benefits are more likely to succeed than those that focus on "negative" issues such as crime, compulsive gambling, and reduced quality of life. As indicated earlier, Dombrink and Thompson's analysis concluded that in only one campaign, New Jersey in 1976, were all of these conditions met.

Between 1988 and 1994, campaigns to legalize land-based or waterborne casinos succeeded in eight states (Iowa, South Dakota, Illinois, Colorado, Mississippi, Louisiana, Missouri, and Indiana) and failed in six states (Ohio, Alaska, Colorado [expansion], Florida, Wyoming, and Rhode Island). With the exception of the Colorado vote to initially legalize land-based casinos in 1990, the veto model was supported in all cases. Those factors predictive of a successful campaign were present in states that legalized casinos (with the exception of Colorado, where legalization occurred despite a lack of support from the governor). At least one factor was absent in states where the campaign failed (Thompson and Gazel, 1995).

Summary

Public policy on gambling is created in a variety of different ways. Legislatures, courts, administrative agencies (especially state gaming commissions), and the electorate all play a role.

The case study of policy making in Wisconsin illustrates a complex process involving many political and business interests. It is anything but a "rational" process, and understanding what happens in one state over even a short period of time requires taking into account what is occurring in nearby states.

The success of a campaign to legalize casino gambling depends on the economic conditions of jurisdictions and their prior experience with other forms of gambling, the support of political and business elites, the credibility and financial resources of proponents, and whether debates are dominated by discussions of potential positive benefits or potential negative problems.

Chapter 7

The Legitimation of The Gambling Industry since the 1970s

The growth of legal gambling in the United States since the 1970s offers a unique opportunity to examine a dramatic social change. Legal gambling—what Skolnick (1978) in his study of Nevada casino gambling called a "pariah industry" has been in the process of developing respectability, social acceptance, and legitimacy. How has this occurred? What fosters the development of respectability? How do previously illegal and deviant activities become transformed into legitimate ones? These are fundamental questions in the study of deviance and social change.

In the mid-1980s John Rosecrance (1988) examined the growth of the legal gambling industry and anticipated the increased social acceptance of gambling that is now well underway. He regarded the spread of casino gambling from Nevada to Atlantic City, state legalization of lotteries, and the ownership of casinos by publicly traded corporations as key factors in the legitimation of gambling. Rosecrance identified some of the variables involved in the legitimation process, but events and expansion of the past decade (riverboat and Indian reservation casinos and the dramatic increase in the amount of money being wagered) require a more thorough and detailed analysis.

Processes of Legitimation

Several factors have contributed to the legitimation of the gambling industry. These include: state legalization; how the gambling industry refers to itself; incorporation of gambling into the entertainment industry; the borrowing of legitimacy from nongambling businesses and occupations; and the way the mass media deal with gambling.

The Role of the State

Probably the most important factor in the transformation of the gambling industry is state legalization of many forms of gambling. When states legalize, license, and tax pari-mutuel racing and land and water based casinos, de facto as well as de jure legitimacy is extended to those activities.

The most dramatic of these events is state operation of lotteries. State run lotteries represent the legal equivalent of illegal numbers (or policy) games, which have been part of American urban life for most of the twentieth century. When states operate lotteries, the state itself becomes part of the gambling industry. So, not only has a previously illegal game (numbers/policy) been made legal, but the bars, candy stores, and barber shops where gamblers once had to go to play a number have been replaced with state-operated outlets. It is difficult to imagine a more dramatic act on the part of government than this—transforming a previously illegal activity into one that has the sponsorship, active encouragement, and blessing of the state.

The state has played other important roles in the legitimation process. Typically, states have created regulatory agencies to oversee the gambling businesses they license, tax, and/or operate. Gaming commissions and boards have become as routine and normal a part of state government bureaucracies as have agencies dealing with licensing drivers, highway repair, insurance regulation, and so on. This routinization of regulatory activities within governmental bureaucratic structures serves to bolster the status of gambling to that of a normal, everyday activity. It also serves to reassure gamblers that games are honest and operated properly, since the state is regulating them (something they could never be sure of when games were operating illegally).

Many state legislatures have also created committees that have oversight responsibility for the operation of the regulatory and licensing agencies. Some of these committees are also responsible for developing new legislation dealing with gambling. Thus, within legislative bodies public policy on gambling assumes the same credibility and importance as matters being dealt with by other committees (such as welfare policy, education funding, highway construction, and natural resource management). Legislative deliberations, hearings, and actions on gambling are routinely covered by the mass media, often with great vigor and interest. As a result, gambling comes to be seen as a routine part of government, lending further legitimacy to it.

As regulatory bodies and legislative committees go about their work, associations and interactions with members of the private gambling industry occur. Public hearings about the impact of existing or proposed gambling enterprises bring gambling industry representatives together with local and state politicians and representatives of nongambling businesses. The result is that the gambling industry becomes incorporated into the political and economic structures of the state and of local communities. The gambling industry also uses the lobbying process to link its interests with the routine activities of legislative bodies.

The motivation for state legalization of gambling has been twofold: to increase revenues and to stimulate economic development. The gambling industry has taken advantage of economic and fiscal crises to promote gambling as a solution to these problems. When local and state politicians considered legalization of gambling along with other revenue generating and economic development proposals, the credibility and legitimacy of gambling is enhanced.

State legalization of gambling has progressed with little organized opposition. When opposition has developed, it often has been a "not in my backyard" response to specific proposals. At other times it has developed as part of a battle over which community in a state will get a proposed gambling business. An exception is Utah, where the Mormon church's opposition to gambling has been the critical factor in the absence of legal gambling in that state. More typically, opposition that does develop tends to be sporadic, poorly funded, and directed toward a particular piece of legislation. Until the mid-1990s, there was no national, organized, sustained opposition to the legalization of gambling. Consequently, there has been no consistent challenge to the growing legitimacy of the gambling industry. This has changed recently, however, with the formation of an antigambling organization called the National Coalition Against Legalized Gambling. The coalition has successfully lobbied in several states against specific initiatives to introduce or to expand gambling.

Some opposition to the legalization of casino gambling (riverboats, Indian reservations) has come from the industry's racing segment. Fear of losing customers to casinos has prompted racetracks to lobby for off-track betting and video poker machines at tracks. Racetracks in West Virginia have added such machines and track owners in Kentucky have lobbied for the addition of casinos to their horse racetracks (Doocey, 1994a). By the early part of 1994, twenty-two states had legalized off-track betting, largely in response to lobbying on the part of racetracks (Doocey, 1994b). This "if you can't beat them, join them" approach has increased the availability, and thereby the legitimacy, of gambling.

When the issue of compulsive gambling has been raised as a negative by-product of legalization, legislatures have responded by allocating money from gambling revenues (usually from lottery profits) for public education about compulsive gambling and for developing compulsive-gambling treatment programs. An example of this occurred in Texas. The legislation that created the Texas Lottery (which began operations in the summer of 1992) allocated $2 million a year from lottery profits for education about and treatment of compulsive gambling. Such actions quiet critics and enable legislators to claim that they are acting responsibly.

Gaming, Not Gambling: The Magic of Words

One way to enhance the status of an occupation that is stigmatized or has low prestige—that is, negative public image—is to change its name. For example, janitors have become custodians, undertakers have become morticians, used-car salespersons have become transportation consultants, and garbage collectors have become sanitary engineers. While name changes of this kind may seem silly, they can affect the way occupations are perceived.

This kind of change has occurred in the gambling industry. Members of the gambling industry don't like the word *gambling* because it conjures up images of illegal activities being conducted by unsavory characters if not by organized crime syndicates. The term *gambling* has been replaced by *gaming,* a somewhat sanitized term for a previously illegal activity. The terms *illegal* and *gambling* are so closely intertwined in legal terminology and popular language that the gambling industry believes the term *gaming* reinforces its now legal and more respectable status.

This change in terminology has occurred at the level of the gambling *industry.* Specific occupations within the industry have not changed their names. Dealers, stickmen, and croupiers still go by these names. This is not to say that casino pit bosses may not some day call themselves "gaming coordinators," but this has not occurred yet.

The euphemism *gaming* is used extensively and occurs in many contexts. Even the federal government has given credibility to the term. The 1988 law establishing the process whereby federally recognized Indian tribes negotiate compacts with the states to operate gambling enterprises is called The Indian *Gaming* Regulatory Act (italics added). This twenty-one-page document does not contain the word *gambling.*

State governments also promote the use of the word *gaming.* The regulatory agencies and legislative oversight committees discussed earlier typically incorporate the term in their titles. When meetings are announced and held, recommendations are made, and reports are issued, "gaming" is publicized and "gambling" fades into the background.

Other examples of the use of the term *gaming* are found in gambling industry publications and trade shows. The major trade publication for the gambling industry is *Gaming and Wagering Business,* established in 1980. Although occasionally the term *gambling* appears, *gaming* tends to be used predominantly throughout the articles that appear in the magazine. Trade shows consistently use the term *gaming*. The largest international gambling event of this kind is held annually in Las Vegas and called "The World *Gaming* Congress and Expo" (italics added).

Another important change in word usage is the use of the terms *wager* and *wagering* instead of *bet* and *betting*. Representatives of the gambling industry show a preference for the term *wager* in their public discussions and publications. Presumably, wagering is not as negative as betting, although the distinction does not seem as strong as that between gambling and gaming. Still, *Gaming and Wagering Business* does have a different ring to it than *Gambling and Betting Business*.

Laws, regulatory bodies, and the gambling industry have helped create a new image of gambling through the use of the terms *gaming* and *wagering*. These changes promote the notion that legal gaming and wagering are qualitatively different than illegal gambling and betting.

More Wordplay: Goodbye Casino, Hello Family Entertainment Complex

Another significant change in terminology has occurred in the way the gambling industry describes the places in which gambling activities occur. The traditional hotel/casino is now referred to as a "family entertainment complex." Casinos have become resorts, with casinos and sports books as part of a larger entertainment menu. This change has occurred in many places, but is most evident on the Las Vegas "Strip."

Circus Circus Enterprises, a major player in the Nevada casino industry, epitomizes this trend. The original Circus Circus located on the Las Vegas Strip, has featured circus acts and midway games since its inception. According to the company, this "entertainment megastore unites elements of a resort hotel, casino, street festival, theater, and theme park under one roof" (Circus Circus Enterprises, 1992: 5). More recent projects, like the Excalibur, with its medieval castle theme, have carried the entertainment complex idea even further. With only a little more than one-fifth of its floor space devoted to casino games, the Excalibur includes nightly jousting contests, a reproduction of a medieval village, Fantasy Faire, and dynamic-motion theaters. Luxor, which opened on the Strip in October 1993, is shaped like a giant pyramid and features activities with Egyptian themes, including "a water journey where visitors will discover artifacts and treasures of ancient Egypt . . . high-tech 'participatory' adventures . . . and replicas of the famed tombs of the Pharaohs" (Circus Circus Enterprises, 1992: 5). MGM Grand and its Wizard of Oz theme, the Mirage and its volcano, Treasure Island and its pirate ship battles, Caesar's Palace and its theme of ancient Rome, New York, New York and its replica of the New York skyline, and others represent this new genre of entertainment destination resorts. While many conventional casinos and casino/hotels remain (especially in downtown Las Vegas but also on the Strip), Las Vegas is clearly being transformed from casinos with a place to sleep to destination resorts in which gambling is but one item on a large entertainment menu (Grossman, 1993; Pierce, 1992).

An appeal to family tourism is an explicit part of the rationale for this emphasis on entertainment and the relative deemphasis of gambling. According to William G. Bennett, Circus Circus Enterprises' chairman of the board and CEO, these entertainment/adventure features of the new theme parks are "specifically for tourists and vacationers, many of whom travel with children these days. Good entertainment is a matter of aiming for the child in all of us" (Circus Circus Enterprises, 1992: 13). Glenn Schaeffer, the company's president, chief financial officer, and treasurer, points out that "a chief growth market for us is the baby-boomer group, who are nearing their peak earning years—and who are coming into their prime family-raising and family-traveling years. . . . A preferred way of spending their family time has become short trips of several days. . . . We need to design and refine projects that appeal as mass-tourism destinations, suitable for tourists, families, and players" (Circus Circus Enterprises, 1992: 14). It is significant that gamblers are referred to as "players." In this imagery, gambling becomes a "game" like others offered in the entertainment theme park.

Combining gambling and theme park resorts is an important part of the legitimation of the gambling industry. The industry is capitalizing on the popularity and wholesome image of resorts and theme parks like Disney World, Six Flags, and Great America. By projecting an image of these new theme parks as places where gambling is secondary to other entertainment, the gambling industry is creating an identity as part of the tourism/entertainment industry instead of the gambling business. As F.M. (Bud) Celey put it, "The new Las Vegas wants to be Disneyland with dice" (cited in Vogel, 1997: 4).

The final example of this process is important because it occurred outside the major places (Nevada and Atlantic City) associated in the past with gambling in the United States. In March 1992, Chicago Mayor Richard Daley announced his support of a proposal from a consortium of three major Nevada casino/hotel corporations (Circus Circus, Caesar's World, and Hilton Hotels) to build a "casino theme park complex" near downtown Chicago. The proposal created a great deal of controversy and generated opposition from many segments of Illinois' gambling industry (riverboat casinos, off track betting, and pari-mutuel racing). What is most important about the proposal and ensuing debate is the rhetoric and imagery that was used.

The project was to have resembled a shopping mall, anchored by four casino/hotels rather than department stores. In addition to shops and

ON THE LAS VEGAS "STRIP" THE EXCALIBUR (TOP) AND NEW YORK NEW YORK (BOTTOM) EPITOMIZE THE NEW WAVE OF ENTERTAINMENT THEME PARKS.

restaurants, the proposal included a sports and performing arts center, a miniature golf course, a skating rink, a high-tech theme park, and an exhibit hall (*Chicago Tribune,* 1992).

In the initial proposal, Daley described the complex as a "project for tourism, gambling, and family entertainment." Glenn Schaeffer of Circus Circus noted that it "would be the first total recreational environment of its kind anywhere in the world" and that "it would be an American playground" (*Chicago Tribune,* 1992). Although the Chicago "mall" anchored with casinos did not come to pass, a conventional shopping mall in Henderson, Nevada, is planning to include a 60,000 square foot casino with 1,800 slot machines, an Olympic-size ice skating rink, and a performing arts center (*Gaming and Wagering Business,* 1997).

Articles and editorials in the major industry trade magazine routinely stress that the future of gambling (world-wide as well as in the United States) lies in the development of entertainment theme parks (*Gaming and Wagering Business,* 1993b). In Nevada, this is done with a clear realization that casino gambling is still the driving economic force in the state. The theme parks may draw people to resort cities like Las Vegas, but they will have failed to serve their purpose if the visitors do not go to the casinos.

The "grind joints" of downtown Las Vegas are not likely to disappear, and the conventional hotel/casinos of Las Vegas and Atlantic City are likely to persist. But as casino expansion and new projects incorporate the theme park motif, the gambling industry as a whole will gain legitimacy from its identification with the tourism/recreation/leisure industry of which it is actively seeking to become a part.

Borrowing Legitimacy

While the gambling industry has borrowed legitimacy from the tourism/recreation/leisure industry, there are a number of other ways legitimacy is acquired. The gambling industry employs and uses the services of professionals from many conventional and prestigious occupations, including accountants, architects and designers, computer technicians, public relations and advertising specialists, as well as providers of food services, security, and financial services. As a legal activity, the gambling industry makes these linkages in an open manner that was impossible when gambling was illegal. Illegal casinos and numbers games operators of the past couldn't advertise in the mass media the way their contemporary legal counterparts do.

The suppliers of services include Bank of America, Ernst and Young, SONY, American Express, Motorola, Panasonic, Eastman Kodak, and MCI Telecommunications. In addition, many casinos, racetracks, and Indian bingo halls make instant cash readily available by honoring credit cards and providing automatic teller machines. VISA, Mastercard, and Discover Card logos are prominently displayed, creating an association with established financial services.

Legitimacy has also been gained through the development of publicly owned corporations within the gambling industry. Industry mainstays such as Circus Circus, Caesar's Palace, Hilton Hotels, Mirage Resorts, Promus, Bally Manufacturing, and International Game Technology are corporations listed on the New York Stock Exchange. Gambling has created broad-based investment opportunities that were unthinkable when the industry was largely illegal. Major investment companies and stock brokerage firms regularly do analyses of the gambling industry for their clients, just as they analyze the investment prospects in petroleum, biotechnology, banking, or soybean futures (Dean Witter, 1992). In 1993, Smith Barney Shearson issued a 125-page analysis of forty-six publicly traded gambling corporations (Ader and Moran, 1993). *Gaming and Wagering Business* provides a monthly summary of the stocks of fifty-seven publicly traded casino operators and twenty publicly traded casino suppliers. National business publications and investment-oriented television programs also routinely analyze and make recommendations about the gambling industry as a place to invest one's money.

The Mass Media

The pari-mutuel segment of the gambling industry has been associated with sporting contests for a long time. The results and schedules of horse and dog races are reported by newspapers on their sports pages. Local television news programs frequently cover horse and dog race results as part of their sports segment. They also routinely provide live coverage of lottery drawings and report winning numbers during news and other programs. Publishing winning lottery numbers in newspapers has become as routine as the daily weather report.

By publishing point-spreads for collegiate and professional football games, newspapers provide important information for gamblers and the (illegal as well as legal) gambling industry. As part of their coverage of sporting events, especially football, television pregame shows commonly feature discussions of the day's odds and point spreads on different games. The experts who provide this information are usually bookmakers who work in Nevada where bookmaking is legal.

By covering racing and sporting events and lottery drawings, the mass media serve to routinize gambling activities and present them as an integral, newsworthy part of social life. In so doing, the mass media contribute to the normalization and legitimation of the legal gambling industry.

Summary

The transformation of the gambling industry from an illegal to a legal activity has been greatly facilitated by actions of the state. Directly through legalization and indirectly through incorporating gambling into the structure of government operations, states have created opportunities for the gambling industry to present itself as a normal, acceptable economic activity.

The legal gambling industry has sought to alter its image by stressing the "play" nature of the "games" it offers to customers. The language used by the industry to describe itself (*gaming* instead of *gambling*) and the redefinition of gambling as a component of the recreation/entertainment/leisure industry are important aspects of this image-changing process.

Externally, legitimacy has been gained through recognition by the investment/brokerage industry and established nongambling businesses and occupations employed by gambling interests. The mass media have also contributed to the legitimacy of the gambling industry through routine coverage of gambling events.

Chapter 8

Changing Perceptions of Gambling

This chapter deals with two topics. First, we will look at attitudes toward gambling. How favorably or unfavorably do people regard gambling? How are the social and demographic characteristics of people related to their attitudes? Have attitudes toward gambling become more favorable over time?

Second, we will look at the kinds of gambling that people participate in and, where data are available, how frequently they engage in different kinds of gambling. We will also examine how social and demographic characteristics are related to gambling participation.

Attitudes Toward Gambling

Given the increase in the availability and accessibility of gambling, it is important to ask if public attitudes toward gambling have become more or less favorable. We would expect attitudes to change in either a positive or a negative direction, depending on people's familiarity and experience with gambling. There is not a great deal of information about attitudes toward gambling to allow us to make comparisons over a long period of time. Still, we can make short-term comparisons.

Information about attitudes comes from both national surveys of the general population and surveys done in single states. Most of the research focuses on attitudes toward specific kinds and forms of gambling (e.g., casinos, lotteries, and so on).

In 1993, the Gallup Organization conducted a survey of 1,016 New Jersey adults for the Council on Compulsive Gambling of New Jersey. Several questions dealt with attitudes toward legalized gambling. Twenty-two percent of the sample believed that gambling was immoral; 66 percent believed that legalization encourages gambling among people who can least afford it; and 61 percent believed that legalization opens the door to organized crime. More than half (57 percent) believed that legalization can lead to compulsive gambling among people who would not gamble illegally. Fifty-nine percent agreed that gambling may undermine the work ethic of young people, and 49 percent believed that gambling teaches young people that you can get something for nothing (Gallup Organization, Inc., 1993).

At the time this survey was done New Jersey had a substantial amount of legal gambling, including a lottery, charitable gambling, pari-mutuel wagering on horses, and twelve major casinos in Atlantic City with a total of 1,288 table games and 24,561 slot machines (*Gaming and Wagering Business,* 1994: 56–57). The survey asked about attitudes toward new forms of gambling, and only 26 percent favored the introduction of new gambling activities. When the survey was conducted, the issue of legalizing sports betting was very much in the news. The sample was almost evenly split on this issue, with 46 percent in favor of legalized sports betting (Gallup Organization, Inc., 1993: 3).

In 1990, a survey of 420 adult Nebraskans asked about attitudes toward gambling in general. Of those who gambled, 82 percent approved of legalized gambling and 62 percent wanted more legal gambling opportunities in the state. Among the nongamblers, 43 percent approved of gambling and a surprising 22 percent wanted more legalized gambling in Nebraska (Abbott and Cramer, 1993).

An Iowa survey in 1996 asked 632 adults a variety of questions about their attitudes toward gambling. Nearly 11 percent opposed all forms of gambling. The survey also found that there was little support for expanding gambling in Iowa. Forty-six percent of the respondents felt that there were too many gambling facilities in the state, 41 percent thought the number was about right, and only 6 percent believed there were too few gambling facilities (Roberts 1996).

A 1997 survey of 401 Wisconsin residents asked about attitudes toward several aspects of gambling. Fifty-two percent of the respondents agreed with the statement "Gambling leads to a decaying of social values"; 45 percent disagreed with the statement. Respondents were almost evenly split on the question of gambling being "a harmless way to produce needed tax revenues for the state"—51 percent agreed and 47 percent disagreed. Perhaps reflecting a pessimistic view of gambling, 68 percent agreed that because people were going to gamble anyway, the state might as well legalize gambling and benefit from tax revenues, while 30 percent disagreed. The most negative perception of gambling emerged in respondents' answer to the statement "Legalized gambling encourages many people to gamble away money they need to support their families." On this issue, 79 percent agreed and 19 percent disagreed (Penaloza, 1997).

Although not strictly attitude studies, research in Texas suggests that many people perceive gambling as entertainment. In 1992—three months prior to and one month following the start of the Texas lottery, 6,308 adults were surveyed about their perception of gambling and their gambling behavior. Sixty-one percent of the sample said that the main reason they gambled was for entertainment. In 1995, a follow-up survey of 7,015 adults was conducted. Entertainment was an "important" or "very important" reason for gambling for 50 percent of this sample. Twenty-nine percent said entertainment was the most important reason that they gambled (Wallisch 1993, 1996). Clearly, this research supports the idea that "entertainment" is a large part of the public perception of gambling.

Another study dealt with 585 residents of three northern Wisconsin counties with access to several of the state's Native American casinos. In 1995, respondents were asked if they were more accepting, less accepting, or unchanged in their view of gambling since it was legalized in Wisconsin. Unfortunately, *gambling* was not explicitly defined. The state legalized a lottery in 1988, and the Native American casinos in the area where the survey was done began operations in 1990 and 1991. Given the locale of the study, it is reasonable to assume that most respondents equated gambling with Native American casinos. Nevertheless, 19 percent of those surveyed had become more accepting of gambling, 32 percent had become less accepting, and 49 percent said that their view of gambling was unchanged (LeFebvre and Kempen, 1995).

Casino Gambling

Information about attitudes toward casino gambling is available from both national and state surveys in the United States and from surveys conducted in Canada and Mexico. Most of the research has asked about attitudes toward "casinos" without specifying a particular type of casino. A few studies have asked specifically about attitudes toward riverboat casinos and casinos on Indian reservations. The results of these surveys are summarized in table 8.1. The questions posed vary according to the different researchers. Differences in wording may affect interpretations of survey results; these will be pointed out.

Beginning in 1992, Harrah's Entertainment, Inc. which operates Harrah's casinos, has conducted an annual survey of casino gambling and attitudes toward gambling using a national panel of approximately 100,000 households. Overall, the proportion of Americans who say that casino gambling is "acceptable for anyone" increased from 55 percent in 1992 to 63 percent in 1996.

During this time period (1990–1996), the proportion of respondents who regarded casino gambling as "acceptable for others, but not for me" decreased from 35 percent to 30 percent. Those who regarded casino gambling as "not acceptable for anyone" remained fairly constant (10 percent in 1992 and 8 percent in 1996).

TABLE 8.1   Attitudes Toward Casino Gambling:
Survey Results

Survey	Location	Year	Sample Size	Percent Favorable/ Approve
General Casino Gambling				
Harrah's	United States	1992	100,000[a]	55
Harrah's	United States	1993	100,000[a]	51
Harrah's	United States	1994	69,449	59
Harrah's	United States	1995	86,806	61
Harrah's	United States	1996	64,500	63
Casino Journal	United States	1994	1,000	54
Gallup	United States	1989	NA	55[b]
Saad	United States	1992	NA	51[b]
Pavalko and Bayer	Virginia	1993	689	52
Harrah's	Canada	1994	505	60
Harrah's	Canada	1995	507	61
Harrah's	Mexico	1994	500	52
Harrah's	Mexico	1995	500	50
Riverboats				
Saad	United States	1992	NA	60
Townsend and Dresner	Wisconsin	1992	500	66
Indian Reservations				
Saad	United States	1992	NA	42
Townsend and Dresner	Wisconsin	1992	500	63

Notes:
a. Number of households contacted. Response rate not reported.
b. Respondents were asked about "casino gambling at resort areas."
NA. Information not available

In 1994 and 1995, Harrah's also surveyed a small sample of Canadians and (mainly middle class) Mexicans (see table 8.1). In 1995, the results for the Canadians were quite similar to those of the U.S. sample, with 61 percent viewing casino gambling "acceptable for anyone" and 10 percent regarding it as "not acceptable for anyone." The Mexican sample expressed somewhat less favorable attitudes, with 50 percent saying that it was "acceptable for anyone." As with the U.S. sample, 10 percent of the Mexicans surveyed also said that casino gambling was "not acceptable for anyone" (Harrah's, 1996: 16).

The U.S. survey also asked about attitudes toward specific gambling issues. In 1996, 52 percent of the respondents indicated that they favored the introduction of casino gambling in their communities because of the economic and tax benefits to the local community. This was up from 39 percent in 1992. In addition, 59 percent agreed that casino gambling brings money into the local economy without hurting existing businesses, a figure 6 percent higher than when the question was first asked in 1993.

The introduction of casinos into communities has some opposition, especially when it comes to locating them near residential areas. Even in Las Vegas, often referred to as a "company town" dominated by the casino industry, residents strongly protested plans in the late 1980s to build casinos oriented toward "locals" near residential areas away from the Strip and its tourist-oriented casinos. In the early 1990s, a survey of 967 Las Vegas residents found strong concern about and opposition to casinos near residential areas. About 65 percent indicated that they wanted to live at least three miles away from a casino (Thompson, et al., 1993).

In the 1996 Harrah's survey, 81 percent of the respondents viewed casino gambling as "a fun night out," compared to 74 percent in 1993, reaffirming the perception of casino gambling as entertainment by the majority of people.

A question put to those surveyed by Harrah's in 1995 (not asked in 1996) was whether or not "the benefits from increased tax revenue and tourist expenditures offset any negative influence of gambling." Fifty-eight percent agreed, up from 48 percent in 1992. The Harrah's survey also asked about attitudes toward the legalization and regulation of gambling. In 1995, 61 percent of the sample agreed that "gambling is harmless fun and the government should make it legal so it can be regulated and taxed." This figure was up from 53 percent in 1992. In the 1996 survey, people were asked their opinion about who should regulate gambling. The overwhelming majority (84 percent) believed that gambling should be regulated by state governments. Thirteen percent favored federal regulation and 3 percent said they didn't know (Harrah's, 1997).

Reflecting Harrah's interest in promoting "responsible gaming," the 1996 survey also asked respondents about their attitudes toward problem gambling and underage gambling. Seventy-eight percent responded that casinos should provide programs that discourage problem gambling, and 85 percent believed that casino companies should have programs to combat underage gambling (Harrah's, 1997).

In 1994, a survey of 1,000 people was conducted for *Casino Journal*, a gambling industry trade magazine (see table 8.1). Respondents were asked,

"In general, do you favor or oppose legalized casino gaming?" Fifty-four percent were in favor, 37 percent were opposed, and 9 percent did not respond.. This is slightly less favorable support for casino gambling than was reported by the Harrah survey and may be due to the difference in wording of the question and the fact that respondents were given a dichotomous choice—in favor of or opposed to (Bet on It!, 1994).

Two Gallup polls, conducted in 1989 and 1992, also provide some information about attitudes toward casino gambling (see table 8.1). The results of these surveys are not strictly comparable to the Harrah's and *Casino Journal* surveys, since respondents were asked only about "casino gambling at resort areas" (presumably Nevada and Atlantic City). Nevertheless, they report a level of favorable support similar to that reported in the other surveys. Favorable responses, however, *decreased* slightly between 1989 and 1992, from 55 to 51 percent (Gallup, 1989; Saad, 1992).

In 1993, a survey of attitudes toward casino gambling was conducted in Virginia. People were asked their views about allowing state licensed and regulated casinos anywhere in the state (Pavalko and Bayer, 1994). As table 8.1 indicates, the majority said that they would "approve," or "somewhat approve" of such a development. This is a positive response toward gambling since, at the time of the survey, the only forms of legal gambling in Virginia were pari-mutuel gambling, lottery, and charitable bingo.

A few studies have addressed attitudes toward riverboat casinos. The national Gallup survey in 1992 did ask about this and reported an approval rate for riverboat casinos of 60 percent (Saad, 1992). A Wisconsin survey also asked about attitudes toward riverboat casinos and found a somewhat higher approval rate of 66 percent (Townsend and Dresner, 1992).

These two surveys also asked about attitudes toward Indian Reservation casinos. The attitudes of Wisconsin residents were much more favorable than those of the general U.S. population. This may reflect Wisconsinites' familiarity with Indian reservation casinos since they are numerous in Wisconsin and in the adjacent states of Michigan and Minnesota.

Overall, these surveys indicate a great deal of support for legalized casino gambling. The trend data that we have covers a relatively short period of time, but it indicates that attitudes toward casino gambling are becoming more favorable.

Lotteries

Both national and state surveys have addressed attitudes toward lotteries. At both the state and national levels, lotteries receive a more favorable endorsement compared to other forms of gambling. In 1989 and 1992, Gallup polls asked a national sample of adults about their attitudes toward lotteries. Seventy-eight percent approved of lotteries in 1989, and 75 percent approved of them in 1992 (Gallup, 1989; Saad, 1992). In the Virginia survey noted earlier, the approval rate (approve or somewhat approve) was 76 percent (Pavalko and Bayer, 1994). The approval rates in the two Gallup surveys and the Virginia survey are somewhat higher than the approval rate of 67 percent found in a 1995 survey of 2,276 Wisconsin residents. The Wisconsin survey also reported that approval of the lottery had declined a bit from 73 percent in 1989 (Piliavin and Rossol, 1995). A 1997 survey that asked Wisconsin residents if the state lottery should be abolished found strong support for the lottery. While 35 percent of the respondents favored abolishing the lottery, 57 percent felt that it should *not* be abolished (Penaloza, 1997).

Off-Track Betting (OTB) and Slots at Racetracks

A 1989 Gallup poll reported that 54 percent of respondents approved of off-track betting (Gallup, 1989). By 1992, approval had dropped to 49 percent (Saad, 1992). In the Virginia study, half of the respondents approved of OTB and of slot machines at racetracks. This was a particularly salient issue in Virginia at the time of the survey, since the issue was under consideration (and later implemented) in neighboring West Virginia.

In a 1992 Wisconsin survey, 37 percent approved of allowing casino gambling at the state's dog race tracks (Townsend and Dresner, 1992). Although the survey asked about "casino gambling" at dog race tracks, public and media discussions of the issue at the time of the survey focused on slot machines and video poker being allowed at tracks. It is likely that respondents had these forms of casino gambling in mind as they answered this question.

Bingo

Three surveys have asked people about their attitudes toward charitable bingo. In the Virginia study, bingo received the strongest endorsement of all the forms of gambling mentioned. Seventy-seven percent approved of this form of gambling (Pavalko and Bayer, 1994). This is similar to the approval rates given to charitable bingo in 1989 (75 percent) and 1992 (72 percent) in the national Gallup surveys (Gallup, 1989; Saad, 1992).

Other Issues

Several other gambling issues have been dealt with in attitude surveys. The national Gallup poll asked about "betting on professional sports such as baseball, basketball, or football." In 1992, 33 percent of respondents approved of this form of gambling, a significant drop from 42 percent in 1989 (Gallup, 1989; Saad, 1992).

In the 1992 Wisconsin survey referred to earlier, 37 percent of the respondents approved of allowing video poker machines in taverns and restaurants. Thirty-nine percent approved of allowing video lottery terminals in taverns and restaurants (Townsend and Dresner, 1992).

Social Characteristics Related to Attitudes Toward Gambling

Four studies have dealt with the relationship between social characteristics and attitudes toward gambling. These include the Virginia survey (Pavalko and Bayer, 1994), the 1992 Gallup Poll (McAneny, 1992) and two Wisconsin surveys focusing on attitudes toward the lottery (Piliavin and Rossol, 1995; Penaloza, 1997).

These studies do not report identical findings, but their results support several broad generalizations. Urban residents have more favorable attitudes toward gambling than rural residents. Men and people under thirty-five are more likely to have positive attitudes toward gambling than women and people over thirty-five. Gambling is regarded more favorably by single people, compared to married and divorced people, except, for lotteries, where marital status is unrelated to attitudes toward the lottery.

Race/ethnicity, income level, and political party affiliation show no consistent relationship to attitudes toward gambling. People with very low and very high levels of education are less likely to approve of gambling than those with moderate educational levels.

Participation in Gambling

Rachel A. Volberg, a sociologist who studies gambling behavior and the prevalence of compulsive gambling, has conducted surveys in more than a dozen states. Her results show that the proportion of the population that has engaged in any form of gambling ranges from about 74 percent in Georgia to 92 percent in New Jersey (Volberg, 1996). In a 1992 Texas survey, 76 percent of adults said that they had gambled at some time in their lives (Wallisch, 1993).

In 1991, a Wisconsin survey of 1,002 adults produced similar results. Seventy-nine percent indicated that they had participated in some form of commercial gambling within the past twelve months (Gray, 1991). A 1997 survey of 401 Wisconsinites found that 66 percent had gambled within the previous year (Penaloza, 1997). In 1990, a slightly lower proportion of Ne-

THE INCREASED AVAILABILITY OF GAMBLING VENUES HAS LED TO
INCREASED PARTICIPATION IN GAMBLING. IN SOUTHERN CALIFORNIA TWO
NATIVE AMERICAN CASINOS, FANTASY SPRINGS NEAR INDIO (TOP) AND
CASINO MORONGO NEAR PALM SPRINGS (BOTTOM) ARE EASILY ACCESSED
FROM I-10, A MAJOR EAST-WEST INTERSTATE HIGHWAY.

braska residents (62 percent) indicated that they had gambled in some form during the previous year (Abbott and Cramer, 1993).

As with attitudes toward gambling, information on specific kinds of gambling participation is available from a variety of sources. These include both national surveys and surveys done in particular states.

Gambling in Casinos

The Harrah's surveys provide a good deal of information about casino gambling. According to Harrah's 1996 survey, at least one person from 32 percent of U.S. households gambled in a casino during 1996, and there were 176 million visits to casinos (Harrah's, 1997). This represents an increase of 354 percent compared to the 46 million visits in 1990. During the period 1991–1996, visits to the "traditional" venues of Nevada and Atlantic City increased by 71 percent, while visits to "new" venues (riverboats, Native American reservation casinos, and casinos in South Dakota and Colorado) increased by 471 percent (Harrah's, 1997). Clearly, the increase in the popularity of casino gambling reflects the increased ease of access and availability created by the expansion of these "new" venues.

Not only has the number of visits to casinos increased, the number of visits per household has also grown. The Harrah's survey reports that the average number of trips per household to casinos was 4.8 in 1995 compared to 2.7 in 1990 (Harrah's, 1997).

The Harrah's surveys also revealed interesting regional patterns in casino gambling. Between 1994 and 1996, the south and the north central regions of the country had much larger increases in the number of casino visits than did the western and northeastern regions (Harrah's, 1996: 19; 1997). In the South, this reflects the growth of riverboat and dockside casinos on the Mississippi River and the Mississippi Gulf Coast. In the north central region, it reflects the increased number of both riverboat and Native American reservation casinos.

The relationship between proximity to casinos and casino visits can be illustrated by looking at the states and cities that serve as the main "feeder markets" for casinos. *Feeder market* refers to a geographic area (city, state) from which casino visitors come. The term is used by casino marketers to identify the places from which casinos are attracting visitors. In 1996, the top ten casino feeder states (in rank order) were California and Illinois (close to Nevada casinos and Illinois riverboats, respectively), Louisiana (close to Louisiana and Mississippi riverboat and dockside casinos), New York and Pennsylvania (close to Atlantic City), Texas (close to Louisiana and Mississippi riverboat and dockside casinos), New Jersey (close to Atlantic City),

Wisconsin (proximity to Native American reservation casinos), Nevada, and Minnesota (proximity to Native American reservation casinos).

The top twenty feeder cities also show a clustering based on proximity to available casinos (table 8.2). Although one would expect large cities such as Los Angeles and New York to be important casino feeders, others in the top twenty list are surprising. In particular, Mobile, Alabama, Pensacola, Florida, and Green Bay/Appleton, Wisconsin, are comparatively small population centers. Their inclusion in the top twenty feeder cities underscores the significance of proximity and availability of gambling facilities to gambling participation.

In 1996, the Harrah's survey identified cities that had more than 500,000 casino visits. The cities included are worth noting because they are unlikely places to produce so many casino visits. They include (with an educated guess at the proximate casino attraction): Flint/Saginaw/Bay City, Michigan; (Michigan Native American reservation casinos and Windsor, Ontario, Canada casino), Johnstown/Altoona, Pennsylvania (Atlantic City), Monroe/El Dorado, Louisiana (Louisiana and Mississippi riverboat and dockside casinos), Springfield/Holyoke, Massachusetts; (Mashantucket Pequot Indian Reservation, Ledyard, Connecticut), and West Palm Beach/Ft. Pierce, Florida. ("cruises to nowhere").

Several of the state surveys discussed earlier also provide information about casino gambling. The Texas surveys found that the percentage of respondents playing casino table games (cards and dice) increased from 8

TABLE 8.2 Top Twenty Casino Feeder Cities, 1996

Casinos Available	Feeder Cities
Nevada	Los Angeles, San Francisco, San Diego, Las Vegas, Phoenix/Flagstaff
Louisiana/Mississippi Riverboats	New Orleans, Memphis, Mobile/Pensacola, Dallas/Ft. Worth
Minnesota/Wisconsin Native American Reservations and Illinois Riverboats	Minneapolis/St. Paul, Milwaukee, Green Bay/Appleton, Chicago
Atlantic City, NJ	New York, Philadelphia
Native American Reservation, Ledyard, CT	Boston
Missouri/Illinois/Mississippi Riverboats	St. Louis, Kansas City, Houston
Michigan Native American Reservations and Windsor, Ontario	Detroit

Source: *Harrah's Survey of Casino Entertainment*, 1997.

percent in 1992 to 13 percent in 1995. In addition, the percentage that played slots or videopoker during the past year increased from 9 percent to 19 percent between 1992 and 1995 (Wallisch, 1996: 17).

A New York state survey of 1,829 people conducted in 1996 found that 51.4 percent had gambled in a casino at some time in their lives. Gambling at "card games" was reported by 36.6 percent, and 11.5 percent reported that they had played "gaming machines." Some of the card game and machine gambling undoubtedly occurred in a casino setting (Volberg, 1996: 11). In the New Jersey survey discussed earlier, 74 percent of the respondents indicated that they had gambled in a casino, 75 percent indicated that they had played slot or videopoker machines, and 19 percent had played dice games. Not specified was whether this gambling occurred in a casino setting (Gallup Organization, 1993: 9).

Surveys in South Dakota and Iowa asked people about casino gambling activities. The 1993 South Dakota survey of 1,767 people found that 47 percent of respondents had, at some time in their lives, played slot machines in South Dakota and 29 percent had played them elsewhere. Twenty-six percent had gambled at card games (not necessarily in a casino), and 9 percent had gambled at dice games (Volberg, 1994: 8). In Iowa, 1,500 people were surveyed in 1995. Fifty-six percent said that they had played slot machines in casinos, 26 percent had played "video gaming devices," and 27 percent had played casino table games (Volberg, 1995: 8). A 1996 Iowa survey found that 43 percent of the respondents had visited a riverboat or land-based casino within the previous year (Roberts, 1996: 5). In 1990, 19 percent of respondents in Nebraska indicated that they had bet in a casino during the past year (Abbott and Cramer, 1993)

The different wording of questions in the various surveys poses a problem in generalizing about casino gambling. Harrah's figure of 31 percent, however, is a good estimate of the national percentage of households in which someone gambled in a casino. State surveys show a wide range of activity, from a low of 13 percent having played cards and dice in Texas to 74 percent in New Jersey having gambled in a casino.

Playing the Lottery

In the national Gallup survey of 1992, 56 percent of the respondents reported buying a state lottery ticket during the past year (McAneny, 1992). State surveys have asked people about lottery ticket purchases for multimillion dollar drawings and for scratch off and pull tab cards with much lower prizes. When we compare the results of these surveys to data on casino gambling, we find that there is great similarity among states in the proportion of people who play the lottery.

Care is needed when examining research on lottery play (and other forms of gambling), since some studies ask respondents if they have ever played, and others ask if they have played in the past year. Obviously, figures for lifetime play will be larger than play within the past year. The results of national and state surveys are summarized in table 8.3.

Three Wisconsin surveys make it possible to look at trends over time (1989 to 1995). As table 8.3 indicates, the percent of people playing the lottery increased slightly between 1989 and 1991, but decreased by 1995. This decrease may be due to Indian reservation casinos opening in the early 1990s.

A 1993 Minnesota survey found that 50 percent of the respondents had played the lottery during the previous two months (St. Cloud State University Survey Research Center, n.d.). In Virginia, 58 percent of the respon-

TABLE 8.3 Lottery Play: Survey Results

Survey	Location	Year	Sample Size	Percent Who Played Lottery Ever	In Past Year
Gallup	United States	1989	NA	—	54
McAneny	United States	1992	NA	—	56
Piliavin and Rossol	Wisconsin	1989	527	—	58
Piliavin and Rossol	Wisconsin	1991	542	—	61
Piliavin and Rossol	Wisconsin	1995	2,084	—	55
Abbott and Cramer	Nebraska	1990	420	—	50[a]
St. Cloud State	Minnesota	1993	NA	—	50
Pavalko and Bayer	Virginia	1993	689	—	58
Wallisch	Texas	1992	6,308	32	17
Wallisch	Texas	1995	7,015	70	57
Volberg (1995)	Iowa	1995	1,500	45	—
Roberts	Iowa	1996	632	—	50
Volberg (1994)	South Dakota	1993	1,767	44	—
Volberg (1993)	Washington	1992	1,502	65	—
Volberg (1996)	New York	1996	1,829	76	—
Gallup Organization	New Jersey	1993	1,016	82	—

Notes:
a. Nebraska did not have a lottery at this time. These probably represent out-of-state lottery ticket purchases.
NA. Information not available.

dents had played the lottery during the past year. In Iowa, 64 percent reported that they had played instant lottery games and 45 percent had played other lottery games. A 1996 survey found that 50 percent of Iowans had purchased a lottery ticket within the past year.

In South Dakota, 44 percent of the people surveyed had purchased at least one lottery ticket. A survey in the state of Washington found that 65 percent of respondents had purchased a lottery ticket at least once in their lives.

In New York state, 76 percent of respondents reported that they had purchased a lottery ticket (Volberg, 1996). In 1993, New Jersey residents reported an even higher rate of lottery play—82 percent.

Frequency of Lottery Play

A national Gallup survey in 1989 found that 23 percent of lottery players bought tickets at least once a week. Of Virginians who play the lottery, 29 percent can be described as frequent lottery players, playing at least once a week (Pavalko and Bayer, 1994).

Both the national and Virginia studies found a much higher rate of frequent play than was found in Wisconsin, where only 9 percent played the lottery once a week or more (Piliavin and Rossol, 1995: 18). In New Jersey, frequent lottery play is much more common, and 40 percent play at least once a week (Gallup Organization, 1993: 11).

Demographics of Lottery Play

The social characteristics of people who play the lottery have been the subject of many studies. These include gender, age, education, income, race/ethnicity, and marital status.

A good deal of research supports the notion that men have traditionally been heavier gamblers than women. Yet, as legal gambling opportunities have grown, women appear to be gambling more (Lindgren, et al., 1987; Lesieur, 1988). However, surveys in Virginia, Wisconsin, Nebraska, Minnesota, New Jersey, and Texas have found that men are more likely than women to play the lottery. The Virginia study also found that men play the lottery more frequently than women.

Conventional wisdom about age and gambling holds that gambling peaks in the twenties, thirties, and forties and tapers off with increasing age, especially after age sixty. Research on age and lottery play generally supports this image. Younger people are more likely than older people to be lottery players, according to research in New Jersey, Virginia, and Wisconsin. Research in Texas, however, found that age was unrelated to lottery play for people under sixty, but after age sixty lottery play declined dramatically (Wallisch, 1996: 16). The Virginia survey (Pavalko and Bayer, 1994) also found that the frequency of lottery play increased with age.

Education is also related to lottery play. Research in both Virginia (Pavalko and Bayer, 1994) and Wisconsin (Paliavin and Rossol, 1995) found that people with less than a high school education and those with college degrees are less likely than others to play the lottery. The Texas survey found that people with a high school education were more likely to play the lottery than those with less or more education. (Wallisch, 1993).

The relationship between income and lottery play has also been studied. In the Virginia survey, lottery play was modestly related to income, with play more frequent among higher income groups. This is consistent with the Wisconsin study, which found increased lottery play at the over $50,000 income level. The Texas survey also found that lottery play was more common among higher income people. In Nebraska, lottery play was higher in the middle income groups ($15,000 to $50,000) than in the lowest (under $15,000) and highest (over $50,000) income groups.

With regard to race/ethnicity and lottery play, research in Virginia found no differences in the rate of lottery play of black and white respondents. Similarly, in Texas, there was no difference in lottery play between white, black, and Hispanic respondents.

In the Virginia survey, no relationship was found between marital status and whether people had played the lottery during the past year. However, frequency of lottery play was related to marital status. Single respondents played less frequently than those who were married, widowed, or divorced. The Wisconsin survey also found no relationship between marital status and lottery play during the past year.

Betting on Horse and Dog Races

Although gambling at racetracks has declined in popularity relative to casino gambling and playing the lottery, it remains an important gambling activity. In the Virginia survey, only 3 percent of the sample had bet at a horse or dog track during the previous year. That is much less than was reported in the 1992 national Gallup survey, where 12 percent reported "betting on a horse race." However, the national data could include respondents who placed bets with bookies. The Texas survey found that 10 percent of the respondents had bet on a horse or dog race in the past year. Half of New Jersey residents surveyed in 1993 reported that they had bet on horse or dog races at least once. However, the question was phrased in such a way that illegal bets with a bookie could have been included.

Surveys done in New York, Washington State, Nebraska, and Iowa reported similar rates—35, 37, 33, and 36 percent, respectively. However, a survey in South Dakota found that only 22 percent of the respondents had gambled on horse or dog races.

Research in Texas found that horse and dog race gamblers tended to be male, Anglo (rather than black or Hispanic), and between the ages of twenty-five and thirty-four. They typically had some education beyond high school and incomes of more than $40,000. In New Jersey, men were more likely than women to bet on horse and dog races (57 percent compared to 43 percent), and people between the ages of thirty-five and sixty-four were more likely to bet than those eighteen to thirty-four and over sixty-five. In Nebraska, men were more likely to bet on horse races, but women were more likely to bet on dog races. The Virginia survey found no relationship between marital status and horse and dog race betting.

Playing Bingo

The 1992 Gallup poll found that 9 percent of the respondents had played bingo for money during the past year. This could have included charitable bingo and bingo at Native American bingo halls. This survey asked people if they had "played bingo for money," and responses could reflect bingo play at Indian reservation bingo halls. In the Virginia study, a little over 6 percent reported playing bingo at a church or other charity during the past year. The Texas survey found that 10 percent had played bingo during the past year, and the 1996 Iowa survey found that 9 percent had played during the past year. Nebraska reported an unusually high rate—21 percent had played bingo within the past year.

Surveys in New York and South Dakota found similar *lifetime* participation rates of bingo play—30 and 34 percent respectively. In an Iowa study, 32 percent reported playing "live bingo or keno" at some time in their lives.

Who are the bingo players? The Virginia study found no significant gender differences in bingo gambling. However, surveys in Texas, North Dakota, Nebraska, and Minnesota found that women play bingo much more frequently than men. The Texas survey also found that bingo players are more likely to be under age thirty-five; Hispanics were more likely than blacks to play bingo, and Anglos were least likely. Bingo players tended to have incomes under $20,000. People with a high school education were more likely to play bingo than those with either less or more than a high school education.

In New Jersey, women were more likely to be bingo players than men (40 percent compared to 28 percent). Bingo gambling was also more common among those age thirty-five and older than it was among people eighteen to thirty-four.

Illegal Gambling

Reliable, systematic information about illegal gambling is hard to come by. Although several surveys have addressed this issue, the findings must be interpreted cautiously. Because respondents may be reluctant to admit to illegal gambling activities (even with assurances of confidentiality and anonymity) illegal gambling is probably underreported.

In the New Jersey survey, 31 percent of the respondents reported that at some time in their lives they had "played the numbers"—the illegal lottery run by criminal syndicates—at least once. Twenty-six percent reported that they had bet on sporting events with a bookie.

The 1996 New York survey found that 28.6 percent of the respondents had bet on sporting events at some time in their lives. Although some of that betting may have occurred at legal Nevada sports books, it seems likely that most of it involved betting with illegal bookies, since sports betting is not legal in New York. In addition, 2.7 percent reported that they had played "the numbers" (Volberg, 1996: 11).

In Texas, only 4 percent of the respondents reported that they had bet on dog or cock fights, gambled in card rooms, or bet on anything through a bookie. In South Dakota, Iowa, and New York, gambling on sporting events was reported by 35 percent, 26 percent, and 29 percent of the respondents, respectively. Betting on sporting events is illegal in these states, so it is safe to assume that most of the betting was done illegally through bookies, although some may have been done legally in Nevada.

Because off-track betting on horse and dog races is widely available, most illegal betting involves sporting events. National and regional telecasts of sporting events have stimulated widespread interest and have contributed to their popularity as something to gamble on. According to Christensen/Cummings Associates, a firm that specializes in research on the gambling industry, approximately $8 billion was illegally bet on sporting events in 1993. By 1995, that figure had increased to an estimated $84 billion. The Council on Compulsive Gambling of New Jersey estimated that this figure would grow to $100 billion for 1997 (McGraw, 1997: 50). Paul Doocey, a writer for *Gaming and Wagering Business,* estimated that, for every dollar legally gambled on sporting events, about $34 is illegally gambled (Doocey, 1996). Money illegally wagered through bookies ultimately ends up in the hands of criminal syndicates and, of course, bypasses the state tax collectors. The gambling industry has long argued for the legalization of gambling on sporting events as a way to increase its revenues as well as state tax revenues.

The National Football League's Super Bowl is the largest single occasion for illegal as well as legal sports betting. In 1995, $69 million was bet legally on the Super Bowl, and an estimated $4 billion was bet illegally (Mc-Graw, 1997: 53). A survey of Wisconsin residents found that 22 percent had bet on the 1997 Super Bowl, a figure that may be inflated because Wisconsin's team, the Green Bay Packers, played in (and won) the game (Penaloza, 1997). While some of those bets may have been placed legally in Nevada and some were probably made between friends, it seems likely that many, if not most, were placed illegally with bookies.

Gambling by young people who are below the legal age for gambling represents a different type of illegal gambling behavior. Although they are playing legal games, it is not legal for them to play the games. In one study by the Massachusetts attorney general's office, eleven girls and ten boys between the ages of nine and seventeen attempted to purchase lottery tickets 153 times. They were successful in 80 percent of their attempts (Harshbarger, 1994). In another study, a sixteen-year-old girl made 100 attempts to purchase lottery tickets and was successful 99 times (Radecki, 1994, 1995). In Illinois, a study by the State Crime Commission reported that two girls, ages twelve and fourteen, purchased lottery tickets on 20 different occasions using vending machines (Zimmerman, 1996).

Information about illegal gamblers is understandably sparse, but some data exist. In New Jersey, illegal gamblers are much more likely to be male (41 percent) than female (13 percent). Illegal betting also decreased with age. In the New Jersey survey, 40 percent of people eighteen to thirty-four had bet illegally, compared to 13 percent of respondents sixty-five and older.

In the Texas survey, young men with higher incomes and education levels were most likely to have bet illegally. No difference was found between the three racial/ethnic groups used in this study (black, white, and Hispanic). Hispanics, however, were more likely to have bet on dog and cock fights, and blacks were more likely to have bet in card rooms. Regardless of race/ethnicity, illegal betting on sports events through a bookie was associated with higher income and education.

Summary

While a small proportion of people oppose gambling, the majority of Americans accept it as a form of entertainment. The majority of Americans have positive, favorable attitudes toward casino gambling, and only 10 percent believe it is not acceptable for anyone (about the same is true in Canada and Mexico). Casino gambling as entertainment is a big part of gambling's favorable image. As casino gambling becomes more available and people are more familiar with it, attitudes toward it become more favorable.

Bingo and lotteries are perceived even more favorably than casino gambling. Off-track betting and racetracks with slot and other machine games receive less support. Gambling on professional sports is viewed more negatively than any other form of gambling.

Most American adults have engaged in some form of gambling at some time during their lives. Approximately one-third of Americans have visited a casino of some kind. Gambling in casinos clearly increases with proximity and accessibility.

Chapter 9

Compulsive Gambling

For most Americans, gambling is a harmless recreational activity. The monthly poker game with friends, the occasional lottery ticket purchase, the weekend outing to a horse or dog racing track, an evening of church bingo, a visit to a casino—in Las Vegas or Atlantic City, on an Indian reservation, on a midwestern riverboat, or on a Caribbean cruise ship—all are popular leisure-time activities that many people enjoy on an occasional and even regular basis. However, for some, gambling is an addiction every bit as real as addiction to alcohol or other drugs. They are compulsive gamblers.

This chapter focuses on understanding compulsive gambling and its complexity. The serious analysis of compulsive gambling is a relatively recent phenomenon. Since the early 1970s, a variety of research and clinical experience has come together to produce a fairly clear picture of compulsive gambling that can best be described as an "illness model."

However, a number of perspectives predate this recent effort. These are reviewed first. Then we look at a more contemporary analysis of compulsive gambling.

Perspectives on Compulsive Gambling

Psychiatrists, psychoanalysts, and psychologists have been interested in compulsive gambling for some time. Their work has produced some interesting, if speculative, interpretations and explanations of compulsive gambling.

Psychoanalysts who study pathological behavior have contributed insights about gambling based largely on their clinical experience with patients. Not surprisingly, they tend to see pathological gambling as rooted in childhood experiences and as a manifestation or symptom of some underlying conflict or neurosis.

Sigmund Freud, founder of psychoanalysis, saw gambling as self-punishment based on guilt that results from Oedipal strivings (the desire to marry one's mother and kill one's father). Freud's interpretation was based largely on his analysis of the life of nineteenth-century Russian novelist Fedor Dostoevski, who was by all accounts a pathological gambler (Freud, 1961).

Other psychoanalysts, following Freud's views on gambling, believed winning symbolizes omnipotence and successful incest, and losing at gambling represents atonement for symbolic parricide (Lindner, 1950). Still others viewed gambling as an escape and defense against severe depression (Niederland, 1967) and as evidence of oral and anal fixations and latent homosexuality (Greenson, 1947).

Another effort to define the characteristics of the pathological gambler in psychoanalytic terms was made by Edmund Bergler (1957). Based on his experience treating pathological gamblers, Bergler identified several key characteristics. These included habitually taking chances to the point where gambling becomes a typical, recurring, and all-consuming activity in the gambler's life. The pathological gambler also has a high level of optimism that is not tempered by defeat; the gambler never "learns a lesson" from losing. Pathological gambling also involves never stopping when one is ahead; when winning, there is the expectation that one will continue to win. Play continues until all the winnings are gone. In a sense, the compulsive gambler is also a compulsive loser. Although pathological gamblers may initially make cautious bets, they inevitably begin risking much more than they can afford to lose. Finally, in Bergler's interpretation, the gambler experiences an intense thrill while gambling that involves a tension between pleasure (winning) and pain (losing).

Bergler believed that gambling that fit this model was evidence of a "dangerous neurosis." The gambler was an objectively sick person but was subjectively unaware of being sick. Although Bergler published this interpretation in 1957, twenty years passed before the "illness model" became the dominant interpretation of compulsive gambling.

There have been a few efforts to empirically test some of the propositions and implications of the psychoanalytic interpretation of compulsive gambling. In the 1920s, Hunter and Brunner (1928) administered the Colgate Personal Inventory of Psychoneurotic Tendencies and the Colgate Personal Inventory of Introversion-Extroversion to a group of heavy gamblers and a control group of nongambling college students. They found no significant differences that would indicate unique personality characteristics among the heavy gamblers. They did find that on both tests the gamblers had a bimodal distribution (that is, scored high or low), while the nongamblers had a distribution close to the normal curve. Just what this difference tells us about the personalities of gamblers is unclear.

In a study of female poker players, McGlothlin (1954) predicted (based on psychoanalytic theory) that his subjects would be emotionally insecure, have a strong belief in luck and superstition, and be risk takers. His subjects completed the Bell Adjustment Inventory and their scores were compared with the scores of the population on which the test had been standardized. The poker players turned out to be better adjusted than the standardization population. However, those poker players with the poorest adjustment were more likely to believe in luck and be superstitious, but they did not take more risks or lose more money than the better adjusted players.

Another test of psychoanalytic hypotheses by Morris (1957) found that, compared to nongamblers, gamblers had a lower sense of self-responsibility and a greater discrepancy between their self-concept and how they thought others saw them. However, the gamblers were no less happy than the nongamblers and were actually more secure.

In another study, members of Gamblers Anonymous, a group of psychiatric hospital inpatients, and a group of "normal" subjects were compared on a number of characteristics linked to psychoanalytic theory. The gamblers were more hostile, aggressive, active, rebellious, "magical" in their thinking, and socially alienated than the normal group (Roston, 1961). When compared to the psychiatric patients, the gamblers were more active, expansive, and facile, but less anxious, worried, and depressed.

The Medicalization of Problem Gambling

Mental health professionals became concerned about problem gambling in the early 1970s. From small beginnings at a Veterans Hospital in Ohio, this concern has grown into a national movement. Psychiatrists, in particular, have worked closely with Gamblers Anonymous in the development of treatment programs (Custer and Milt, 1985). It is quite clear that problem gambling has become "medicalized," that is, it has come to be seen as a "disease," despite the fact that this way of viewing problem gambling has its critics (Blaszcsynski and McConaghy, 1989; Blume, 1987; Dickerson, 1987; Rosecrance, 1985). Consequently, physicians (mainly psychiatrists) and psychologists have developed a monopoly over the definition of the nature of problem gambling and the nature of the appropriate treatment for it.

Among psychiatrists, psychologists, and a wide array of counselors working in the area of mental health and drug addiction, compulsive gambling has come to be seen as an addiction. The very use of the term *compulsive* conveys the idea of a loss of control over one's behavior and an uncontrollable urge to gamble regardless of the psychological, interpersonal, and financial consequences. One of the leading authorities on the topic, psychiatrist Robert Custer, defined compulsive gambling as "an addictive illness in which the subject is driven by an overwhelming uncontrollable impulse to gamble. The impulse progresses in intensity and urgency, consuming more and more of the individual's time, energy, and emotional and material resources. Ultimately, it invades, undermines, and often destroys everything that is meaningful in his life" (Custer and Milt, 1985: 22). Thus, although no "substance" is involved, the definition parallels that of drug (including alcohol) addiction.

Still, there is an unsettled debate about the nature of compulsive gambling *as an addiction.* It is not a physiological addiction like addiction to alcohol or other drugs, since no external substance is taken into the body. Yet, it is appropriate to describe compulsive gamblers as *psychologically* addicted to, or at least dependent on, gambling (Walker, 1989).

What Is Compulsive Gambling?

The American Psychiatric Association (APA) considers pathological gambling to be an impulse control disorder in which there is a chronic and progressive failure to resist impulses to gamble.

Although the APA uses the term *pathological*, the terms *compulsive* and *pathological* are often used interchangeably when discussing gambling disorders. Professionals who treat compulsive gamblers tend to use the term *pathological*, since pathological gambling is an "impulse control disorder" and not a "compulsion" (Lesieur, 1998b).

The term *problem gambler* is used in two different ways. First, it is used to refer to people who develop family, work, or financial problems as a result of their gambling but do not exhibit all of the characteristics of pathological gamblers. In other words, they have less-serious problems than pathological gamblers have. The term *problem gambler* also is used in a more inclusive way to capture both pathological/compulsive gambling at one extreme and any problematic involvement with gambling at the other end of the continuum (Cox, et al., 1997; Lesieur, 1998b). The distinction is similar to those that we find in the area of alcoholism. While not all problem drinkers are alcoholics, those who are alcoholics certainly have a problem with drinking. Similarly, while not all problem gamblers are pathological/compulsive gamblers, pathological/compulsive gamblers are problem gamblers (Lesieur, 1998b). In this chapter, the terms *compulsive gambler* or *compulsive gambling* are used except in a quotation and where research is being summarized that distinguishes between pathological gambling that meets the APA diagnostic criteria and problematic gambling that does not meet those criteria.

Compulsive gambling has also been described as "a progressive disorder characterized by a continuous or periodic loss of control over gambling; a preoccupation with gambling and with obtaining money with which to gamble; irrational thinking; and a continuation of the behavior despite adverse consequences" (Rosenthal and Lesieur, 1992). This, in essence, is a definition of an addiction.

The APA first recognized compulsive gambling as a mental disorder in 1980 in the third edition of its *Diagnostic and Statistical Manual of Mental Disorders* (DSM-III). In the fourth edition of this manual, published in 1994 (DSM-IV), ten criteria are used to define pathological gambling. According to the APA, a person must exhibit at least five of these criteria to be diagnosed as a compulsive gambler (American Psychiatric Association, 1994). These criteria are presented in figure 9.1 and are used as a framework for developing an understanding of compulsive gambling and compulsive gamblers.

Like alcoholics and drug addicts, compulsive gamblers have an intense *preoccupation* with gambling. It is the focus of their lives, often to the exclusion of other interests. Compulsive gamblers are unable to control the amount of money they gamble or the amount of time they spend gambling.

Like alcoholics and other drug addicts, compulsive gamblers develop *tolerance*. As tolerance develops, they increase the amount they wager in order to achieve the desired excitement. They also escalate from simple to exotic wagers, where the risks and potential winnings are great. Rather than a simple bet on a horse to win a race, they bet the daily double, quinellas, or trifectas. Rather than a simple "pass line" bet, the craps player takes the high risk—high payoff "proposition" bets in the center of the craps table layout.

Like chemically dependent people, compulsive gamblers experience *withdrawal symptoms* when they attempt to limit or stop their gambling. When gambling opportunities are not available or when they do not have money with which to gamble, compulsive gamblers get irritable, nervous, and restless.

When they lose, compulsive gamblers *"chase"* their losses in an attempt to get even or recoup what they have lost. This is an extremely important characteristic that distinguishes recreational gamblers from compulsive gamblers (Lesieur, 1984). Most nonaddicted gamblers can rationalize their losses without further consequences. They may regard their losses as the cost of their entertainment, or they may say that they chose to gamble rather than spend their money on an evening out—dinner, the theater, and so on. Compulsive gamblers cannot do that. They make every effort to return to gambling as soon as they can (as soon as they have obtained more money) to try to win back what they have lost.

Compulsive gamblers *lie to family and friends* about their gambling activities, their losses, and their gambling debts. They attempt to keep their

FIGURE 9.1   DSM-IV Diagnostic Criteria for Pathological Gambling

1. Preoccupied with gambling (e.g., preoccupied with reliving past gambling experiences, handicapping, or planning the next venture, or thinking of ways to get money with which to gamble).
2. Needs to gamble with increasing amounts of money in order to achieve the desired excitement.
3. Restlessness or irritability when attempting to cut down or stop gambling.
4. Gambles as a way of escaping from problems or relieving dysphoric mood (e.g., feelings of helplessness, guilt, anxiety, or depression).
5. After losing money gambling, often returns another day in order to get even ("chasing one's losses").
6. Lies to family members or others to conceal the extent of involvement with gambling.
7. Illegal acts (e.g., forgery, fraud, theft, embezzlement) are committed in order to finance gambling.
8. Has jeopardized or lost significant relationship, job, or educational or career opportunity because of gambling.
9. Reliance on others to provide money to relieve a desperate financial situation caused by gambling (a bailout).
10. Repeated unsuccessful efforts to control, cut back, or stop gambling.

Source: Reprinted with permission from the Diagnostic and Statistical Manual of Mental Disorders, Fourth Edition. Copyright 1994 American Psychiatric Association.

gambling, their losses, and their gambling debts a secret as long as possible. They construct elaborate lies and charades to conceal their activities and related problems.

When opportunities arise or when their financial situation becomes desperate, compulsive gamblers engage in *illegal activities* in order to obtain money for gambling or to pay off gambling debts. They eventually become mired in a cycle of indebtedness in which they are constantly seeking funds to pay off their debts and continue their gambling.

In three studies of members of Gamblers Anonymous (GA) that included a total of 394 people in Illinois, Wisconsin, and Connecticut, 56.6 percent admitted to stealing in various ways to finance their gambling (summarized in Lesieur, 1998a). The total amount of money stolen by these people was $30,065,812—an average of $76,309 per person. One had stolen $8 million and another had stolen $7.5 million.

A study of 306 Australian compulsive gamblers found that 59 percent had committed at least one gambling-related crime during their gambling careers. The most common crimes were larceny, embezzlement, misappropriation of funds, breaking and entering, and shoplifting. Armed robbery, drug dealing, and other crimes were less frequently reported (Blaszcznski and McConaghy, 1994).

To What Is the Compulsive Gambler Addicted?

While the similarities between compulsive gamblers and alcoholics and other drug addicts are striking, compulsive gamblers do not ingest, inject, or inhale chemical substances. Just what is it that they are addicted to? The answer appears to be "action." Action has been described in many ways. It is an aroused, euphoric state. It involves excitement, tension, and anticipation over the outcome of a gambling event. It is the thrill of living "on the edge," of having one's fate riding on the turn of a card or the roll of the dice. Compulsive gamblers have described action as a "high" similar to that experienced from cocaine, heroin, or other drugs. Some report these sensations as they anticipate engaging in a gambling activity as well as when they are actually gambling.

Compulsive gamblers describe action as a "rush" that may include rapid heartbeat, sweaty palms, even nausea. One compulsive gambler I talked with described his first big win—$600 on a long shot at Arlington Race Track near Chicago—this way: "It was as if a bolt of lightning went off in my brain. Looking back [over a gambling career of twenty years], from that moment on, I was hooked. I keep trying to get that lightning bolt to go off again."

Compulsive gamblers often describe being in action as "better than drugs and better than sex." When they are in action, compulsive gamblers lose track of time, and ordinary physical needs take a back seat to the quest for action. They have been known to go for extended periods of time without sleep, food, water, or using a bathroom. Compulsive gamblers have reported experiencing trancelike disassociative states in which they lose track of time and have out-of-body experiences (Jacobs, 1989a).

Cross-Addiction and Addiction Switching

A good deal of evidence supports the idea that chemical dependency and compulsive gambling are related. This is called *cross-addiction.*

Research studies involving members of Gamblers Anonymous and compulsive gamblers in treatment have found that between 47 and 52 percent of these gamblers have had a serious chemical addiction (usually alcohol) at some point in their lives and frequently for a long period of time (Lesieur, 1998b). In addition, studies of people receiving inpatient treatment for alcohol and other drug addiction have found that between 9 and 14 percent are compulsive gamblers (Lesieur, 1984, 1998b; Lesieur and Heineman, 1988; Lesieur and Rosenthal, 1991).

Addiction switching also occurs. The evidence for this consists mainly of reports by counselors who have found that about 10 percent of recovering alcoholics replace their alcohol use with gambling, and about the same proportion of recovering compulsive gamblers become heavy consumers of alcohol (Blume, 1994).

A Canadian study provides different evidence of a link between gambling and other addictions. This study of 2,016 adults found that heavy gamblers were more likely to binge drink and smoke than were light and moderate gamblers or nongamblers (Smart and Ferris, 1996).

Compulsive Gambling and Mental Health

Compulsive gamblers have a high incidence of insomnia, intestinal disorders, migraine headaches, and other stress related disorders. Studies of members of GA have found an especially high incidence of depression—between 70 and 76 percent have been diagnosed as suffering from depression by a mental health professional at some time in their lives (Lesieur, 1998b). Whether they gamble to relieve depression (as the DSM-IV criteria suggest) or whether depression is a result of their gambling (indebtedness, marital conflicts, job loss) is an unresolved issue.

In many respects compulsive gambling is a hidden addiction. Few members of GA reported that they were referred to GA by a mental health professional. Those who had been treated by psychiatrists, psychologists, and other counselors for mental health problems reported that they were rarely asked about their gambling behavior.

Although compulsive gambling is similar to chemical dependency in many ways, it is much more difficult to detect because there are no physical signs as there are with addiction to alcohol or other drugs. You can't smell compulsive gambling on someone's breath. A compulsive gambler's eyes don't dilate. Dice, chips, and cards don't leave marks on the gambler's arms. Compulsive gambling doesn't make you walk funny, stagger, and fall down in a stupor the way excessive alcohol consumption can.

Studies of GA members also have found that between 13 and 24 percent have attempted suicide because of their gambling problems. This attempted suicide rate is six times higher than that of the general population. A survey of 162 GA members found that 13 percent had attempted suicide and an additional 21 percent had considered it (Frank, et al., 1991). It is significant that the suicide rate in Nevada is the highest of any state in the country and about three times the national average.

Personality Characteristics of the Compulsive Gambler

If there is a "compulsive gambling personality type," it has yet to be identified in a precise manner. However, compulsive gamblers do exhibit some distinctive characteristics. While these are commonly found among compulsive gamblers, it must be remembered that not every compulsive gambler will exhibit all of them or exhibit them in an extreme way. There is considerable diversity among compulsive gamblers. Some are action seekers, drawn to gambling for the excitement it offers. Others are escape gamblers, who use gambling as an escape from a variety of personal problems.

Compulsive gamblers tend to be very intelligent, energetic, hard working people who enjoy challenging tasks (such as handicapping races or sporting events). They also tend to be narcissistic, arrogant, and very self-confident (Taber et al., 1986). They believe that they have the power to beat the laws of probability. They see themselves as winners and others as losers or suckers. They also value the attention and recognition that comes from being perceived as a winner by others.

Compulsive gamblers have a need to control events, and gambling provides the illusion that they can control the uncontrollable. Some develop a kind of "irrational thinking" in which they come to believe that they can (literally) control the turn of a card, the roll of the dice, the spin of a wheel, or the outcome of a race. In the advanced stages of this disorder, especially when they see their financial problems as unsolvable and they become desperate, compulsive gamblers begin thinking "backwards" about their problems. Rather than seeing their financial, family, work, legal, and other problems as a *result* of their gambling, they see further gambling as the *solution* to their problems. "If only I had money to gamble with, I could win some money, and all my problems would be taken care of" is the all too familiar complaint of the compulsive gambler.

There is also evidence that compulsive gamblers are self-centered, insecure, and tend to exhibit a disregard for authority. They are highly competitive, but seem to have abandoned or given up on conventional ways of competing. One interpretation is that, because compulsive gamblers have doubts about the strength of their personal resources, they turn to gambling in an attempt to be successful (Graham and Lowenfeld, 1986). This perspective is consistent with Merton's (1957) idea that when people do not have access to conventional and socially approved means for achieving success, they will become "innovative" and turn to deviant means of achieving the goal of success. On some standardized personality tests, compulsive gamblers appear to be quite similar to alcoholics (Ciarrocchi et al., 1991).

Compulsive Gambling and Criminal Behavior

Compulsive gamblers borrow money from friends, relatives, co-workers, banks, loan companies, credit unions, credit cards, and loan sharks in order to pay their gambling debts and stay in action. In several studies, the average gambling-related debt of male compulsive gamblers was estimated at between $42,000 and $54,000, excluding home mortgages, car loans, and other consumer loans (Council on Compulsive Gambling of New Jersey, 1991; Blackman et al., 1986). The level of indebtedness is approximately one-third lower for female compulsive gamblers (Lesieur, 1988).

Given their indebtedness and the desire to stay in action, it is not surprising that compulsive gamblers engage in a variety of illegal behavior. About two-thirds of compulsive gamblers report that they have engaged in illegal activities to pay gambling debts or obtain money with which to gamble (National Council on Problem Gambling, no date). The illegal activities reported include forgery, embezzlement, fraud, tax evasion/fraud, and a variety of "street crimes."

A study of prisoners in a northeastern state in the mid-1980s shed additional light on the link between compulsive gambling and crime. A total of 348 prisoners (230 males and 118 females) admitted to committing the following crimes *in order to finance their gambling or pay gambling debts*: 54 percent of men and women had sold illegal drugs; 56 percent of women had forged a check, 42 percent had fenced stolen goods, and 39 percent had engaged in prostitution; 47 percent of men had committed burglary and 50 percent had taken part in a con game. About 10 percent of these prisoners believed that they were compulsive gamblers, and 13 percent said that their gambling was related to the reason they were in prison (Lesieur and Klein, 1985).

The commission of crimes by compulsive gamblers is often a matter of opportunity and interpersonal contacts. For example, those who bet on races and sporting events with illegal bookies may become bookies themselves or "runners" for bookies in order to obtain gambling money or pay off gambling debts (Lesieur, 1984).

In June 1992, I met a sixty-year-old woman in Cleveland, Ohio, who had spent about $250,000 over a two-year period playing church bingo. She was employed as a part-time bookkeeper for a construction firm. Her work gave her the opportunity to embezzle $75,000 from her employer to finance some of her gambling activities.

Assessment and Diagnosis of Compulsive Gambling

Gamblers Anonymous has developed a list of 20 Questions based on over forty years of experience working with compulsive gamblers. GA's questions are presented in figure 9.2. In many ways these questions are similar to the DSM-IV criteria. According to GA, a compulsive gambler will answer "yes" to at least seven of these questions.

FIGURE 9.2   Gamblers Anonymous 20 Questions

1. Did you ever lose time from work due to gambling?
2. Has gambling ever made your home life unhappy?
3. Did gambling affect your reputation?
4. Have you ever felt remorse after gambling?
5. Did you ever gamble to get money with which to pay debts or otherwise solve financial difficulties?
6. Did gambling cause a decrease in your ambition or efficiency?
7. After losing did you feel you must return as soon as possible and win back your losses?
8. After a win did you have a strong urge to return and win more?
9. Did you often gamble until your last dollar was gone?
10. Did you ever borrow to finance your gambling?
11. Have you ever sold any real or personal property to finance gambling?
12. Were you reluctant to use "gambling money" for normal expenditures?
13. Did gambling make you careless of the welfare of your family?
14. Did you ever gamble longer than you had planned?
15. Have you ever gambled to escape worry or trouble?
16. Have you ever committed, or considered committing, an illegal act to finance gambling?
17. Did gambling cause you to have difficulty in sleeping?
18. Do arguments, disappointments, or frustrations create within you an urge to gamble?
19. Did you ever have an urge to celebrate any good fortune by a few hours of gambling?
20. Have you ever considered self-destruction as a result of your gambling?

Source: Gamblers Anonymous, P.O. Box 17173, Los Angeles, CA 90017.

In the mid-1980s a compulsive gambling screening instrument was developed by Henry R. Lesieur, a sociologist, and Sheila B. Blume, a psychiatrist, at the South Oaks Institute of Alcoholism and Addictive Behavior Studies in Amityville, New York (Lesieur and Blume, 1987, 1993). A copy of this instrument, along with the scoring sheet, is presented in figure 9.3. The South Oaks Gambling Screen (SOGS) has become the standard tool for identifying compulsive gamblers. It has been translated into ten languages and is widely used in survey research and for clinical diagnosis. This instrument can be self-administered or the questions can be asked of the subject by an interviewer.

Not all questions on the SOGS are scored (questions 1 to 3, 12, 16j, and 16k are not counted). Questions 1 to 3, 16j, and 16k provide information about the extent and variety of a person's involvement with gambling. Question 12 sets the stage for question 13, which *is* scored. The maximum possible score is 20. A score of 5 or higher indicates that a person is probably a pathological (compulsive) gambler. A score of 1 to 4 indicates that a person has a gambling problem but does not have sufficient symptoms to be considered a

FIGURE 9.3   South Oaks Gambling Screen

Name _____   Date _____

1. Please indicate which of the following types of gambling you have done in your lifetime. For each type, mark one answer: "not at all," "less than once a week," or "once a week or more."

Not at all	Less than once a week	Once a week or more	
a. _____	_____	_____	play cards for money
b. _____	_____	_____	bet on horses, dogs, or other animals (at OTB, the track, or with a bookie)
c. _____	_____	_____	bet on sports (parlay cards, with a bookie, or at Jai Alai)
d. _____	_____	_____	played dice games (including craps, over and under, or other dice games) for money
e. _____	_____	_____	gambled in a casino (legal or otherwise)
f. _____	_____	_____	played the numbers or bet on lotteries
g. _____	_____	_____	played bingo for money
h. _____	_____	_____	played the stock, options, and/or commodities market
i. _____	_____	_____	played slot machines, poker machines, or other gambling machines
j. _____	_____	_____	bowled, shot pool, played golf, or some other game of skill for money
k. _____	_____	_____	pull tabs or "paper" games other than lotteries
m. _____	_____	_____	some form of gambling not listed above please specify_____

2. What is the largest amount of money you have ever gambled with on any one day?

_____ never have gambled   _____ more than $100 up to $1,000
_____ $1 or less   _____ more than $1,000 up to $10,000
_____ more than $1 up to $10   _____ more than $10,000
_____ more than $10 up to $100

3. Check which of the following people in your life has (or had) a gambling problem.

_____ father   _____ mother   _____ brother or sister   _____ grandparent
_____ my spouse/partner   _____ my child(ren)   _____ another relative
_____ a friend or someone else important in my life

4. When you gamble, how often do you go back another day to win back money you lost?

_____ never
_____ some of the time (less than half the time I lost)
_____ most of the time I lost
_____ every time I lost

5. Have you ever claimed to be winning money gambling but weren't really? In fact, you lost?

_____ never (or never gamble)
_____ yes, less than half the time I lost
_____ yes, most of the time

FIGURE 9.3   (continued)

6. Do you feel you have ever had a problem with betting money or gambling?

    _____ no
    _____ yes, in the past but not now
    _____ yes

7. Did you ever gamble more than you intend to?.............. _____ yes _____ no

8. Have people criticized your betting or told you that you had a gambling problem, regardless of whether or not you thought it was true?................................. _____ yes _____ no

9. Have you ever felt guilty about the way you gamble or what happens when you gamble? .... _____ yes _____ no

10. Have you ever felt like you would like to stop betting money or gambling but didn't think you could?.............. _____ yes _____ no

11. Have you ever hidden betting slips, lottery tickets, gambling money, I.O.U.s, or other signs of betting or gambling from your spouse, children, or other important people in your life?... _____ yes _____ no

12. Have you ever argued with people you live with over how you handle money? .... _____ yes _____ no

13. (If you answered yes to question 12): Have money arguments ever centered on your gambling? .... _____ yes _____ no

14. Have you ever borrowed from someone and not paid them back as a result of your gambling? .... _____ yes _____ no

15. Have you ever lost time from work (or school) due to betting money or gambling?... _____ yes _____ no

16. If you borrowed money to gamble or to pay gambling debts, who or where did you borrow from? (check "yes" or "no" for each)

	no	yes
a. from household money...	( )	( )
b. from your spouse...	( )	( )
c. from other relatives or in-laws	( )	( )
d. from banks, loan companies, or credit unions	( )	( )
e. from credit cards...	( )	( )
f. from loan sharks...	( )	( )
g. you cashed in stocks, bonds, or other securities	( )	( )
h. you sold personal or family property	( )	( )
i. you borrowed on your checking account (passed bad checks)...	( )	( )
j. you have (had) a credit line with a bookie	( )	( )
k. you have (had) a credit line with a casino.................................	( )	( )

(continued)

FIGURE 9.3 (continued)

South Oaks Gambling Screen Score Sheet

Scores on the SOGS itself are determined by adding up the number of questions which show an "at risk" response:

Questions 1, 2, and 3 not counted

Question 4 — most of the time I lose
    or
    every time I lose

Question 5 — yes, less than half the time I lose
    or
    yes, most of the time

Question 6 — yes, in the past but not now
    or
    yes

Question 7 — yes
"   8 — yes
"   9 — yes
"   10 — yes
"   11 — yes
"   12 not counted
"   13 — yes
"   14 — yes
"   15 — yes
"   16a — yes
"   16b — yes
"   16c — yes
"   16d — yes
"   16e — yes
"   16f — yes
"   16g — yes
"   16h — yes
"   16i — yes
questions 16 j and k not counted

Total _____ (there are 20 questions which are counted)

0 = no problem

1-4 = some problem

5 or more = probable pathological gambler

Source: Lesieur, Henry R., and Blume, Sheila B., 1993, "Revising the South Oaks Gambling Screen in Different Settings," *Journal of Gambling Studies,* 9 (Fall), pp. 213–219. Used by permission.

compulsive gambler. The questions on the SOGS are typically asked on a "life-time" basis but can also be asked for shorter time periods (past year, past six months).

Clearly, the questions on the SOGS reflect the DSM-IV criteria and are similar in many ways to GA's 20 Questions. Researchers who have assessed the same people by means of two or three of these instruments report high correlations between them.

The Prevalence of Compulsive Gambling among Adults in the United States

Just how big a problem is compulsive gambling? What proportion of the population consists of compulsive gamblers? These are frequently asked questions, especially by policymakers considering legalizing new gambling venues or debating the merits of proposals to provide funding for public education about compulsive gambling or the treatment of compulsive gambling. Research on the prevalence of compulsive gambling among both adults and youth is reviewed in this section.

Only one *national* study has attempted to determine the prevalence of compulsive gambling. It was conducted in 1974 by the University of Michigan's Institute for Social Research for the Commission on the Review of National Policy Toward Gambling. The study found that 0.77 percent of the American adult population (approximately 1.1 million people) could be considered "probable compulsive gamblers" (Kallick et al. 1979). The study is dated, having been done well before the dramatic expansion of gambling in the 1980s and 1990s. It cannot be regarded as an accurate estimate of the prevalence of compulsive gambling today.

However, since the mid-1980s, a number of state surveys have been conducted, typically at the initiative of state lottery boards and gaming commissions. These surveys are sufficient in number and have been done in such a variety of states and regions that they provide a reliable estimate and picture of the prevalence of compulsive gambling throughout the United States.

Table 9.1 presents a summary overview of this research, with survey results grouped by region. In most surveys a distinction is made between "probable compulsive gamblers" (those who score 5 or higher on the South Oaks Gambling Screen) and "problem gamblers" (those who score 3 or 4 on the SOGS). In table 9.1 and the discussion that follows, these two groups are combined and will be referred to as "problem gamblers."

TABLE 9.1 Lifetime Prevalence Rates for Problem Gambling

Region and State	Year	Sample Size	Prevalence Rate (%)
Northeast			
New York	1986	1,000	4.2
New York	1996	1,829	7.3
New Jersey	1988	1,000	4.2
Maryland	1988	750	3.9
Massachusetts	1989	750	4.4
Connecticut	1991	1,000	6.3
Midwest/Central			
Iowa	1989	750	1.7
Iowa	1995	1,500	5.4
Minnesota	1990	1,251	2.4
Minnesota	1994	1,028	4.4
South Dakota	1991	1,560	2.8
South Dakota	1993	1,767	2.3
Montana	1992	1,020	3.6
North Dakota	1992	1,517	3.5
West			
California	1990	1,250	4.1
Texas	1992	6,308	4.8
Texas	1995	7,015	5.4
Washington State	1992	1,502	5.1
South			
Georgia	1994	1,551	4.4
Louisiana	1995	1,818	7.0
Mississippi	1996	1,014	6.8

Sources: Cox et al., 1997; Emerson and Laundergan, 1996; Volberg, 1995; Volberg, 1996; Wallisch, 1996.

Some surveys also make a distinction based on peoples' response to the SOGS questions for different time frames, such as "lifetime," "the past year," or "the past six months." In table 9.1, all prevalence rates are for *lifetime* responses on the SOGS.

If we take an average of these prevalence rates, we find that about 4.3 percent of the adult population are problem gamblers. In 1995 there were just under 187 million people in the United States age twenty and older (U.S. Bureau of the Census, 1996). If the rate of problem gambling is 4.3 percent, that translates into a little over 8 million problem gamblers.

Several important patterns are evident in the data in table 9.1. Prevalence rates tend to cluster into two groups. In the Midwest/Central region, with comparatively little gambling, prevalence rates tend to be lower than in the other regions. For example, in 1989, Iowa had a low prevalence rate (this survey was done two years before riverboat casinos began operating). The other regions (Northeast/West/South) have higher prevalence rates. Especially noteworthy are Connecticut, with greater accessibility to gambling (an Indian tribal casino), and Louisiana and Mississippi, where riverboat gambling has become widespread in recent years.

Another pattern involves changes over time in the prevalence rate of particular states. As the data in table 9.1 indicate, there are five states in which "replication" studies have been done (New York, Iowa, Minnesota, South Dakota, and Texas). The results of these replications are somewhat mixed, but they indicate a pattern. The largest increase in the prevalence of problem gambling occurred in New York and Iowa. During the time period covered, Iowa experienced a substantial increase in the availability of legal gambling. The time period between the original baseline study and the replication study was also longer for these two states than the other three (ten years for New York and six years for Iowa). Minnesota experienced the next highest increase in the prevalence of problem gambling (2.0 percent). In Texas the increase was small (0.6 percent), and in South Dakota the prevalence of problem gambling actually decreased by 0.5 percent. In Texas and South Dakota, only three years elapsed between the original study and the replication studies, and the negligible differences may be a result of this short time period.

In general, these patterns support the notion that the more available and accessible gambling is, the higher the prevalence of problem gambling.

The Prevalence of Compulsive Gambling among Adults in Other Societies

Prevalence studies have been done in other societies. In Canada, studies have been carried out in six of the ten provinces. Research done between 1989 and 1993 used the South Oaks Gambling Screen or modifications of it. Researchers used the same (or similar) scoring criteria that were used in studies done in the United States. The prevalence of problem gambling in Canada appears to be similar to that in the United States. For example, in Quebec and Saskatchewan "lifetime" prevalence rates of 3.8 and 4.0 percent, respectively, were found. In New Brunswick, Nova Scotia, Alberta, and Saskatchewan, using responses "for the past year," problem gambling prevalence rates of 4.5, 4.7, 5.4, and 2.7 percent, respectively, were found. In the survey conducted in Ontario, a prevalence rate of 8.6 percent was reported (Ladouceur, 1996), but it is not clear whether the time frame used was "lifetime" or "past year."

Prevalence studies have also been carried out in Australia and New Zealand. In Australia, a 1991 survey of 2,744 people in four state capitals (Sydney, Melbourne, Adelaide, and Brisbane) concluded that problem gamblers constituted 1.16 percent of the population. This relatively low prevalence rate is not comparable to the findings of studies done in the United States, since respondents were asked to answer the questions on the South Oaks Gambling Screen using "the past six months" as their time frame (Dickerson, et al., 1996).

In New Zealand, a 1991 survey of 3,933 people found a somewhat higher rate of problem gambling. Using "the past six months" time frame, 3.3 percent of the New Zealand population can be considered problem gamblers. However, when "lifetime" problem gambling was assessed, the prevalence rate was 6.9 percent, a figure consistent with the results of research done in the United States (Abbott and Volberg, 1996).

Research on the prevalence of compulsive gambling was conducted in Spain in the early 1990s using the South Oaks Gambling Screen. Based on studies conducted in four regions of the country, the rate of problem gambling (scores of 3 or higher on the South Oaks Gambling Screen) appears to be about 4 percent (Becona, 1996).

No comparable prevalence surveys thus far have been done in other European countries. However, for Germany and Holland, information exists that is suggestive of the existence of problem gambling in these countries. In the German state of Bavaria, for example, 30,000 people have banned themselves from casinos. In 1987, 3,400 people attended Gamblers Anonymous meetings, and in 1988, 4,900 people with problems related to slot machine gambling sought advice or treatment from Gamblers Anonymous (Becona, 1996).

Somewhat more indirect data from Holland suggest that problem gambling occurs in that society, too. There are seventeen alcohol and drug treatment centers located in Holland. The number of people seeking help at these centers for gambling-related problems rose from 10 in 1985 to 3,883 in 1991 (Becona, 1996).

In late 1997, Howard Schaffer and his associates (1997) completed a review of 120 published and unpublished prevalence studies conducted in the United States and Canada. They analyzed studies of the general population and "special populations" such as prisoners, college students, and youth. They designated three levels of gamblers. Level 1 includes people who gamble with no adverse consequences. Level 2 gamblers are those whose gambling produces a range of adverse consequences, but they do not meet the criteria for Level 3. At Level 3 are gamblers who meet the diagnostic criteria for pathological gambling. The researchers refer to these as "disordered gamblers." They concluded that, based on "lifetime" prevalence, disordered (Level 3) gamblers make up 1.60 percent of the general adult population. For Level 2 gamblers, the lifetime prevalence rate was 3.85 percent in the general adult population. This review also concluded that the rate of disordered (Level 3) gambling has been increasing over time.

The Prevalence of Compulsive Gambling among Youth

In most jurisdictions it is illegal for anyone under the age of eighteen to gamble, and in some states the age at which people can gamble legally is twenty-one. Yet, gambling is commonplace among young people. A survey of 332 Atlantic City high school students in the mid-1980s found that the percent of students who had gambled in Atlantic City casinos increased from 42 percent of fourteen-year-olds to 88 percent of nineteen-year-olds (Arcuri et al., 1985). In a review of five studies of gambling among high school students, Jacobs (1989b) reported that 40 to 86 percent had gambled for money within the past year. The review concluded that the rate of compulsive gambling among high school students was at least three times higher than it was among adults.

In the late 1980s, a survey of 1,771 students at five colleges found that over 90 percent of males and 82 percent of females had gambled at some time in their lives. About a third of the males and 15 percent of the females gambled at least once a week (Lesieur et al., 1991). This study concluded that the level of compulsive gambling among college students was eight times higher than it was in the general adult population.

One difficulty in actually measuring compulsive gambling among youth is the fact that the main screening instruments (the South Oaks Gambling Screen and GA's 20 Questions) are worded for adult respondents. Consequently, questions posed to young people have had to be reworded. In the early 1990s, researchers at the University of Minnesota developed a revision of the South Oaks Gambling Screen that has come to be known as the SOGS-RA (revised, adolescent) (Winters et al., 1993a). While it retains the concepts and focuses on the same behaviors as the SOGS, the questions are phrased in a way that is applicable to the lives, activities, and experiences of youth.

Schaffer and Hall (1996) conducted a review and synthesis of eleven studies of adolescents in five major regions of the United States and Canada. While the studies they reviewed used different measures (DSM-IV criteria, GA's 20 Questions, SOGS-RA) and terminology, they concluded that the rate of compulsive/pathological/problem gambling among adolescents ranges between a low of 0.9 percent (Washington state) and a high of 8.7 percent (Minnesota). Based on five of the studies reviewed, they concluded that there is an additional subgroup of young people who are "at risk" or have a "high risk" of developing a serious gambling problem. That group ranges in size from 9 percent to 17 percent.

The review of 120 prevalence studies discussed earlier (Schaffer et al., 1997) also analyzed studies of prevalence rates among college students and other youth. The reviewers concluded that the rate of Level 3 "disordered" gambling was 4.67 percent among college students and 3.88 percent among youth. The prevalence rate for gambling at what the reviewers call Level 2 (gambling with adverse consequences but not meeting the diagnostic criteria for pathological gambling found at Level 3) was 9.28 percent among college students and 9.45 percent among youth.

Some research suggests that risk-taking behavior is associated with sensation-seeking among children and adolescents. In a study of 115 third through eighth graders, Miller and Byrnes (1997) found that students who scored high on measures of thrill- and adventure-seeking were more likely to select the riskiest options in tasks involving skill and in games involving chance. This relationship held at all grade levels and was not related to gender or competitiveness.

Alcohol and drug use among youth have been the focus of a great deal of attention in recent years, including research, legislation, treatment programs, and educational programs. Comparatively little attention has been given to adolescent problem gambling. Just as getting served in a bar is exciting and gains one prestige among one's peers, so does gambling at a casino or a race track. In some respects, gambling has been added to alcohol and drug use in youth culture rites of passage to adulthood. Gambling is illegal, adults and other authority figures say you shouldn't do it, it's risky and exciting, and you can brag to your friends about having done it. It should not surprise us that, like experimentation with other exciting and risky behaviors, gambling is an appealing activity for many young people (Winters et al., 1993b). And like the adults whose behavior they may seek to emulate, young people develop gambling problems.

The Social Costs of Compulsive Gambling

A variety of social costs are associated with compulsive gambling. They include costs to individuals, their families and friends, costs to financial institutions, costs to the human service and criminal justice systems of society, and costs to the employers of compulsive gamblers.

Costs to the Individual

The psychological costs of compulsive gambling to individuals are enormous. By the time they get to the point of seeking help for their gambling problem, compulsive gamblers are heavily in debt, may have lost their jobs, are likely to be experiencing depression, and have seriously considered (and possibly attempted) suicide. Depression and anxiety are commonplace reactions to gambling-related problems. Compulsive gamblers are also likely to have withdrawn from social contact with others and feel both guilty and helpless as they confront their problems.

Studies have found that between 21 and 36 percent of Gamblers Anonymous members have lost their jobs because of their gambling (Ladouceur et al., 1994; Meyer et al., 1995; Lesieur and Anderson, 1995; Thompson et al., 1996). The financial costs incurred by compulsive gamblers are devastating. Heavily mortgaged homes and businesses, bankruptcy, and money owed to friends, banks, loan companies, credit card companies, the Internal Revenue Service, loan sharks, bookies, and casinos all represent indebtedness from which there is no easy way out. Studies of members of Gamblers Anonymous indicate that from 18 to 28 percent of men and 8 percent of women have declared bankruptcy (Lesieur, 1997). Recent studies of Gamblers Anonymous members in Wisconsin and Illinois found that at the time they entered GA they had gambling-related debts averaging $38,664 in Wisconsin and $113,640 in Illinois (Thompson et al., 1996; Lesieur and Anderson, 1995).

Costs to Families

Having spent years (even decades) lying to family members about their gambling and financial problems, compulsive gamblers have strained relationships with spouses, children, and other relatives. In those marriages that do not end in divorce, spouses and children are likely to experience resentment and confusion about the material deprivations that the family may have undergone as a result of the compulsive gamblers' expenditures. With compulsive gamblers' lives revolving around gambling and getting money for gambling, immediate family members often feel ignored and rejected. A student of mine described her ex-husband, a compulsive gambler who bet on college and professional football games. She said he "disappeared" in August as he began handicapping games for the beginning of the season and "reemerged" in February following the Pro Bowl game. Of course, he didn't really disappear, but handicapping, betting, and following the results of games was such an all-consuming activity that, for all practical purposes, he was not a participating member of the family.

As a result of financial problems and emotional absence and neglect, compulsive gamblers' marriages often end in separation or divorce. Both the emotional and financial costs of separation and divorce need to be acknowledged. Gamblers Anonymous members in Wisconsin and Illinois report that between 26 and 30 percent have experienced gambling-related divorces or separations (Thompson et al., 1996; Lesieur and Anderson, 1995). Compulsive gamblers' families are less cohesive and independent than families of alcoholics and other drug addicts. They function more poorly than families in the general population in terms of problem solving, communication, and taking on responsibilities (Ahrons, 1989; Ciarrocchi and Hohnmann, 1989; Epstein, 1992).

It was noted earlier that case studies indicate that compulsive gamblers are more likely than the general population to attempt suicide. A national study of actual suicides provides additional evidence of a link between gambling and suicide. Using data from the U.S. National Center for Health Statistics for the period 1969-1991, David Phillips and his associates (1997) compared the Las Vegas, Reno, and Atlantic City Standard Metropolitan Statistical Areas (SMSA) with the rest of the United States. They examined suicides among both visitors and residents. Nationally, the average rate of visitor suicides as a percent of all visitor deaths was 0.97 percent. For Las Vegas, the rate was 4.28 percent, the highest in the country. Reno's and Atlantic City's rates (2.31 and 1.87 percent, respectively) were also well above the national average. In the case of Atlantic City, the visitor suicide rate was not higher than that of similar communities before the opening of casinos in 1978. However, after casinos opened, the visitor suicide rate became unusually high. Among residents during the three-year period 1989 to 1991, Las Vegas and Reno had the highest suicide rates in the country, and the rate for Atlantic City was significantly above the national average. This study also found no support for the interpretation that gambling settings "attract" suicidal people, either as visitors or as residents. Phillips and his associates concluded that the risks of suicide are elevated for gamblers and for the spouses and children of gamblers visiting gambling communities and for gamblers and their spouses and children who reside in such communities. They also cautiously pointed out that the increased expansion and availability of legalized gambling may be accompanied by an increase in suicides.

The wives of compulsive gamblers have been found to have an attempted suicide rate about three times higher than that of married women in the general population (Lorenz and Shuttlesworth, 1983). Probably as a reaction to the frustrations of dealing with a compulsive gambler, about 37 percent of spouses of compulsive gamblers have physically abused their children (Lorenz, 1981).

Not a great deal is known about the children of compulsive gamblers. However, there is some research suggesting that, compared to their peers, they have lower academic performance in school, are more likely to have drug, gambling, and eating disorders, and are more likely to be depressed (Jacobs, 1989b; Jacobs, 1989c). Other research found inconsistent support for this conclusion. Children from "multiproblem" families (including compulsive gambling) seem to exhibit more of these problems than those from families with only a compulsive gambling parent. Children of compulsive gamblers who have participated in treatment programs also are less likely to exhibit problems than those who have not been involved in treatment and recovery programs (Lesieur and Rothschild, 1989).

Costs to Financial Institutions

Banks, loan companies, credit unions, credit card issuers, and insurance companies all incur costs generated by compulsive gamblers. Pursuing unpaid loans and mortgages, collecting payments, garnishing wages, conducting foreclosure proceedings, and dealing with fraudulent claims all cost these companies time and money.

Costs to Human Service Agencies and the Criminal Justice System

When they become desperate, compulsive gamblers and their families may turn to human service agencies for food stamps and assistance from general welfare programs. Unemployment and disability benefits may also be used for gambling or to pay gambling debts.

A good deal of attention has been given in recent years to "deadbeat parents" who fail to make payments for the support of their dependent children following divorce. Information is not available on the extent to which this problem is exacerbated by compulsive gamblers, but it seems reasonable that they are related. Pursuing deadbeat parents is a cost for human service agencies in the form of the time and effort of employees spent trying to obtain payments.

The criminal justice system also incurs costs related to compulsive gambling. Compulsive gamblers commit crimes to get money with which to gamble and pay their debts. The cost of trials and incarceration for those crimes is borne by the criminal justice system. Lesieur and Anderson report that in their study of 184 Gamblers Anonymous members in Illinois, fifty-six admitted stealing. While one member stole $7.5 million, the average amount stolen was $60,700 (Lesieur and Anderson, 1995). In a Wisconsin survey of Gamblers Anonymous members, 46 percent admitted stealing, including one person who stole $8 million. The average amount stolen was $5,738 (Thompson et al., 1996).

Costs to Employers

As employees, compulsive gamblers create costs for their employers as a result of tardiness, absenteeism, and theft. They seek advances on their pay and may spend time trying to borrow money from co-workers. They may gamble at work, spending time on the phone with a bookie or arranging loans and trying to put off creditors. They also are likely to take extended lunch hours and breaks, especially if they work with minimal supervision. Above all, they are distracted and not likely to be conscientious, productive employees. Concentrating on their gambling and related money concerns is their first priority. Compulsive gamblers often add to the cost of employer sponsored health insurance premiums because of the stress-related illnesses they experience due to their gambling. Several studies have found that between 69 and 76 percent of compulsive gamblers have missed time from work (absence, tardiness) because of their gambling (Ladouceur et al., 1994; Meyer et al., 1995; Lesieur and Anderson, 1995).

Summary

Recognition of pathological gambling as a mental disorder by the American Psychiatric Association in 1980 was a landmark event in the medicalization of compulsive gambling. While there is debate, most descriptions and analyses of compulsive gambling treat it as an addiction, stressing similarities with alcohol and other drug addiction. In particular, tolerance, withdrawal, and preoccupation with gambling are symptoms similar to those found in people addicted to alcohol and other drugs. Lying about gambling, borrowing money to cover debts and stay "in action," and chasing losses are other distinguishing characteristics of compulsive gamblers.

As compulsive gambling progresses, family relationships deteriorate and employment is jeopardized. Compulsive gamblers may turn to crime to get money with which to gamble or to pay off debts. They are also more likely to attempt suicide than the general population.

Research of the prevalence of compulsive gambling indicates that between 3 and 6 percent of the population can be described as compulsive or problem gamblers. Research in the United States and in other countries suggests that prevalence rates are directly related to the availability and accessibility of gambling.

The South Oaks Gambling Screen is the most widely recognized and used instrument for identifying compulsive gambling. The 20 Questions developed by Gamblers Anonymous and the American Psychiatric Association's diagnostic criteria are also important assessment tools.

The social costs of compulsive gambling include costs to both individuals and families. In addition, financial institutions incur the costs of dealing with bad debts and unpaid loans. The criminal justice and human service systems must absorb the costs associated with dealing with compulsive gamblers who have committed gambling-related crimes and with families experiencing gambling-related problems. Finally, employers deal with costs associated with absenteeism and tardiness on the part of distracted employees who give more attention to their gambling than to their work.

Chapter 10

The Treatment of Compulsive Gambling

Compulsive gamblers do not readily seek treatment. Seeking help is an admission of failure, an admission that their gambling fantasies are just that—fantasies. They may also have failed to get help from counselors or Gamblers Anonymous, and failed at efforts to control or cut back on their gambling. The very idea of getting help for a gambling problem is often viewed with a great deal of ambivalence. Treatment may not work and may turn out to be just another failure. At the same time, they fear that if treatment is successful, they may have to give up (in effect, "lose") what could well be the most exciting or comforting activity in their lives (Taber, 1985). Moreover, for compulsive gamblers, giving up gambling means leaving the world of fantasy to which they have escaped and confronting the problems and realities associated with everyday living in the real world.

When compulsive gamblers do seek treatment, it is often because something dramatic has happened in their lives, and they may feel coerced or blackmailed into seeking help. A spouse may have threatened or filed for divorce, or just have left. When asked why they decided to go to a Gamblers Anonymous meeting, it is not uncommon for people to say that their spouse said, "It's GA or *go!*" Others have been arrested for a crime, or a crime such as embezzlement has been discovered by an employer or business partner, and "getting help" is a condition of not filing criminal charges. A bank may have foreclosed on a mortgage. A bookie wants his money *now!* A suicide attempt may have failed, or a seriously contemplated suicide may prompt a search for help.

In addition to such fears and ambivalence, compulsive gamblers go for long periods of time denying that they have a gambling problem. Despite enormous and repeated financial losses, loss of employment, extreme indebtedness, and loss of family and friends, denial can be strong and persistent. Compulsive gamblers live in a fantasy world where the big win that will solve all their problems is just around the corner, just another bet away.

Denial of a problem is undoubtedly the major obstacle to treatment. Counselors with experience in the treatment of both alcoholics and compulsive gamblers contend that the denial of a problem by compulsive gamblers is more intense than that of alcoholics. There are a number of reasons for this. While there are many similarities between alcoholism and compulsive gambling, there are also some differences when it comes to the ease with which the problem can be denied. Unlike the alcoholic who rarely has a "good drunk," compulsive gamblers can have "good days," when they leave a casino or a race track as winners. For the moment, their lives are in order, and they see no problem. As pointed out in chapter 9, compulsive gamblers do not exhibit the obvious kinds of physical signs and symptoms of addiction that alcoholics do. Consequently, it is easier for them to explain financial and other difficulties as due to something other than a "gambling problem."

Finally, compulsive gambling lacks public awareness and understanding as a disorder. Our culture lacks a vocabulary for recognizing, understanding, and explaining compulsive gambling as a disorder like the vocabulary that has developed over the past fifty years for alcoholism.

According to Richard Rosenthal and Loreen Rugle (1994), who have treated compulsive gamblers, when compulsive gamblers seek treatment, they offer a variety of explanations for their gambling. Understanding these explanations is crucial for developing a treatment plan. Compulsive gamblers need and desire spectacular success as a way of demonstrating their worth and gaining approval from others. Anger and rebellion are other explanations they offer. When they are angry at someone, they gamble to punish the other person, with the expectation that the person will be humiliated when the gambler wins. Part of the attraction of gambling is also that it is a way of expressing rebellious, anti-authority feelings.

Gambling is a way of gaining freedom from dependence on others. Some compulsive gamblers believe that if they could win enough to quit their job or get a divorce, they would no longer be subject to the whims of others. Rosenthal and Rugle (1994) argue that compulsive gamblers often confuse potential financial independence with emotional independence from others.

Compulsive gamblers gamble in order to gain social acceptance. Many compulsive gamblers report feeling good when they get "perks" when gambling in casinos. They also enjoy a sense of kinship with other gamblers, bookies, and casino or track personnel because it makes them feel included and a part of something.

Gambling is also a way of escaping from painful or intolerable feelings. Rosenthal and Rugle (1994: 30) describe this as a kind of "self-medication," where gambling may function as an antidepressant or to prolong and intensify the manic phase of bipolar (manic/depressive) disorder (Rosenthal and Rugle, 1994: 30).

A final explanation for gambling has to do with competitiveness. Rosenthal and Rugle point out that compulsive gamblers are highly competitive. Often as a result of trying to impress and please parents, competitiveness develops into a trait expressed in many situations. For some, gambling becomes a competitive activity in which losing is unacceptable or even unthinkable, and the potential for "chasing losses" becomes enormous.

Treatment Issues

Treatment involves changing compulsive gamblers' lifestyle—helping them develop new interests, activities, and ways of thinking and behaving. Since many compulsive gamblers use gambling as a way of escaping from problems encountered in their lives, they need to acquire new problem solving skills.

No single "one size fits all" treatment exists for compulsive gambling. Treatment strategies are based on a variety of individual and group therapies and participation in Gamblers Anonymous. Custer's explanation of the origins of compulsive gambling stresses unmet needs for approval and recognition, and a lack of confidence in one's ability to deal effectively with life's problems (Custer and Milt, 1985: 70). Many treatment strategies are based on this perspective.

A basic issue in treatment is what the goal of treatment should be. Some counselors take the approach that the goal of treatment should be the complete cessation of gambling activities. This is essentially the goal of Gamblers Anonymous, which seeks to help compulsive gamblers live free of gambling. In effect, the goal is to replace gambling with *not gambling* as the dominant feature of the compulsive gambler's life. Other counselors stress the need to deal with the basic causes of compulsive gambling. The strategy in this approach is to deal with the motivations for gambling, the problems related to gambling, and the psychodynamics of gambling behavior.

A related issue in compulsive gambling treatment is whether total abstinence from gambling is essential, or whether it is possible for compulsive gamblers to scale back their gambling and become "controlled" (recreational) gamblers. Gamblers Anonymous takes the position that abstinence is essential. The vast majority of compulsive gambling counselors also hold this perspective. John Rosecrance, a critic of the conventional "medical model" interpretation of compulsive gambling, has argued that, for many problem gamblers, abstinence may be an unrealistic (and unnecessary) goal (Rosecrance, 1988). Other researchers, both sociologists and psychologists, have taken the position that the "loss of control" implied by the terms *compulsive gambling* and *pathological gambling* is overstated and misplaced.

Research on gamblers in natural settings and experiments designed to teach problem gamblers to gamble in a controlled way suggest that there are other options than total abstinence in treating compulsive gambling (Dickerson, 1984; Dickerson et al., 1979; Hayano, 1982; Oldman, 1978; Rankin, 1982; Scott, 1968). This issue is similar to the debate that has developed regarding whether or not it is possible for alcoholics to become "controlled" drinkers (Fingarette, 1988).

Treatment Models

The strategies used by counselors and treatment programs are varied, and particular counselors and programs use different approaches with different clients. There are four main approaches to treatment: aversion therapy, behavioral counseling, desensitization, and cognitive-behavioral therapy. Lesieur (1998) has provided a concise overview of these approaches and has summarized the small amount of research that has been done on their effectiveness. The research evaluating these treatment strategies shows mixed and inconsistent results, due in large part to the small size of the samples used. Following are some of the main characteristics along with features that are common to most treatment strategies and programs.

An early part of treatment involves educating the compulsive gambler about the nature of this disorder. Compulsive gamblers are often confused about what has happened to them. They lack a vocabulary that can help them understand the nature of their behavior and the attendant problems. "Why did this happen to *me*?" or "What's wrong with me?" are common reactions of compulsive gamblers. An important part of this educational process is emphasizing that "you are not alone," that other people are experiencing the same kinds of problems with their gambling.

Typically, compulsive gamblers have serious financial problems. Before a treatment program can begin to address the "gambling problem," some semblance of order needs to be brought into the financial aspect of a gambler's life. In addition to owing money to friends, relatives, credit card issuers, finance companies, loan sharks, bookies, and others, it is not unusual for compulsive gamblers to owe money to the Internal Revenue Service (and its state equivalents) for unpaid taxes and to face foreclosure on their home mortgage or business loans. The legal implications of these problems are so serious that the involvement of a lawyer may be necessary. Assistance from an experienced financial counselor may also be needed to develop repayment plans for outstanding loans. If financial fraud, embezzlement, or forgery have been committed, legal assistance and advice is also essential.

Another part of dealing with the compulsive gambler's finances is setting up a realistic and workable budget. Often this requires turning over complete control of family income to a spouse and putting the gambler on an allowance. As might be expected, this tends to be strenuously resisted since it severely limits access to gambling money and places the gambler in a dependent, childlike status. Moreover, it represents a dramatic change in terms of the extent to which the gambler is in control of her or his life.

A related aspect of dealing with finances is developing a "restitution plan" for paying back what is owed to relatives, friends, co-workers, and others. It often requires tactful negotiation with the people to whom the money is owed. On the one hand, compulsive gamblers find this embarrassing, since it involves admitting to others the extent of their gambling problem and their inability to control it. On the other hand, it is valuable because it forces gamblers to confront the extent and seriousness of the financial problems that exist and the impact that gambling has had on others.

By the time compulsive gamblers seek help, it is quite likely that their jobs are in jeopardy. Absenteeism, tardiness, lack of attention to work responsibilities, and borrowing from co-workers are all likely to make the compulsive gambler less than a valuable employee. Consequently, it is often necessary to inform an employer of the nature of the gambling problem that exists. Understandably, compulsive gamblers are resistant to doing this, but it is essential if the gambling problem is going to be addressed in a comprehensive way.

Many compulsive gamblers are dually addicted. Besides being compulsive gamblers, they are also addicted to alcohol or other drugs. In such cases, treatment needs to address the alcohol/drug problem as well as the gambling problem.

Treating compulsive gambling involves more than just treating the gambler. It necessarily includes treating the gambler's family. Issues such as money-management clearly involve the spouse and often other family members.

The gambler's spouse and children are often as confused as the gambler about the nature of what has been going on. They also need education and information about the nature of compulsive gambling.

Spouses typically engage in a great deal of denial of the problem, explaining the gambler's behavior as temporary. Frustration and resentment mount as unpaid bills pile up, creditors become more insistent, and the gambler's inability to control his or her gambling becomes more evident. Having lied and hidden the problem from friends and family, a spouse is likely to have withdrawn from others in order to avoid embarrassment. He or she also may have considered divorce or separation as a way of dealing with the problem.

In some cases a spouse may become depressed and ineffective at work and as a parent. A vague sense of distress, confusion, and anxiety are common. In extreme cases, thinking becomes impaired and inability to function in normal roles occurs. As Joanna Franklin and Donald Thoms, counselors with experience in the treatment of compulsive gamblers and their families, put it, the spouse "may feel helpless and hopeless, may be abusing substances (especially alcohol and pills), considering divorce, suffering from depression, and in the extreme, considering suicide" (1989: 138). Individual counseling for the spouse, and marriage and family counseling for the entire family, are needed in many cases. One study of spouses of compulsive gamblers identified them as angry, depressed, isolated from the gambling spouse, guilty, suicidal, and experiencing a variety of stress-related physical symptoms including headaches, insomnia, and various aches and pains (Lorenz and Yaffee, 1989).

It is reasonable and logical that treatment strategies should be based on a sound understanding of how and why people become compulsive gamblers. In a major review of treatment programs and strategies, Alex Blaszczynski and Derrick Silove, Australian researchers, pointed out that "there is no comprehensive model of gambling available that effectively explains the pathogenic process leading to the transition from controlled to pathological gambling, its persistence and maintenance over time, and why relapse occurs after periods of abstinence/control" (1995: 196). Consequently, there is great variety in existing approaches to managing and treating compulsive gambling that range from single therapies to combinations of specific therapies, some having as their goal abstinence from gambling and others striving to achieve controlled gambling.

Blaszczynski and Silove's review of research on the effectiveness of well over a dozen different therapies concluded that there are certain key components to the successful treatment of compulsive gambling. The therapist's job would be to assure that these conditions are met. They include:

1. In order to reduce the risk of relapse, the compulsive gambler should avoid exposure to gambling cues and situations and exposure to other gamblers.
2. Stress management techniques need to be used to lower arousal and anxiety and to serve as a more appropriate way of coping than gambling.
3. If the compulsive gambler is experiencing "dysphoric mood" (i.e., is depressed), antidepressants may need to be prescribed by a physician.
4. Illogical and erroneous beliefs, attitudes, and expectations regarding gambling need to be challenged and corrected, with an emphasis placed on preventing relapse.
5. Marriage counseling may be needed to reestablish trust between partners.

6. Budgeting skills and acceptance of financial responsibility need to be developed with a concern for meeting financial obligations without gambling (this is essentially what was referred to earlier as "restitution").
7. Nongambling leisure activities must be developed.
8. Addiction to alcohol and other drugs needs to be addressed if this is present.
9. Attendance by the gambler at Gamblers Anonymous meetings and by his or her spouse at GamAnon meetings is essential.

Gamblers Anonymous

The vast majority of counselors regard involvement in Gamblers Anonymous (GA) as essential for successful recovery. According to Gamblers Anonymous, the Fellowship of Gamblers Anonymous was founded in 1957 in Los Angeles by a recovering alcoholic and compulsive gambler known as Jim W. He was joined in this effort by another gambler, Sam J. However, this starting date is in dispute. According to other unofficial accounts, it began in 1947 (Browne, 1994; Deland, 1950). What became of this initial effort is unclear, but the GA that began in 1957 has been in operation continuously since that time.

GA is a private, nonprofit organization that exists for the purpose of helping compulsive gamblers live their lives free of gambling. GA groups are self-supporting and do not accept outside contributions. There are more than one thousand chapters worldwide.

The GA recovery program is a "12 Step" program similar to that of Alcoholics Anonymous (AA), which started in 1935. Some GA chapters are also informally affiliated with inpatient and outpatient treatment programs operated by Veterans Administration hospitals, psychiatric hospitals, and a wide variety of addiction treatment and counseling programs. The overwhelming majority of compulsive gambling counselors encourage and even insist that their clients actively participate in GA. Because GA does not record attendance and gambling activities of its members (it takes the anonymity seriously), it is extremely difficult to evaluate how successful it is in helping its members achieve recovery. Two other groups are affiliated with GA: GamAnon for family members and friends of compulsive gamblers, and GamaTeen for the teenage children of compulsive gamblers.

Given Jim W.'s familiarity with AA as a recovering alcoholic, it is not surprising that the GA recovery program is modeled after AA's "12 Step" recovery program. However, it differs from the AA program in several important ways. One minor difference is that GA meetings tend to be longer than AA meetings, largely because GA meetings provide an opportunity for everyone to "give therapy" by talking about their (and others') gambling problems. In most communities, GA meetings tend to occur less frequently than AA meetings. Also, GA places less emphasis on systematically working through the steps. Consequently, there tend to be fewer step meetings (Lesieur, 1990; Browne, 1991).

GA's strength lies in its reinforcement of the idea that the compulsive gambler's problems are shared and experienced by other people. That is what makes it a self-help *group*. How it accomplishes that involves what Browne (1991) has called a "selective adaptation" of the AA model. Compared to AA, GA has a different perspective on "spirituality." AA's 12 Steps make frequent reference to God (for example, "Made a decision to turn our will and our lives over to the care of God as we understand Him," "Admitted to God, to ourselves, and to another human being the exact nature of our wrongs"). GA's 12 Steps make less frequent reference to God ("Admitted to ourselves and to another human being the exact nature of our wrongs") and when the word *God* is used, it tends to be qualified in various ways. According to Browne (1994), one of the reasons for this is that Sam J. (Jim W.'s collaborator in the 1957 founding of GA) was an atheist.

Another important difference between AA and GA recovery programs is their fundamental conception of the addiction problem that their members are dealing with. From the AA perspective, alcoholism is the *symptom* of an underlying problem having to do with the person's character (self-centered, self-praising, or self-loathing). GA, on the other hand, *sees gambling as the problem.* The AA program places considerable emphasis on the goal of developing self-understanding, reflection on the self, and coming to grips with character flaws once abstinence from alcohol has been achieved. In GA, achieving abstinence from gambling is the goal, and there is much less discussion of feelings about and perceptions of one's self than there is in AA. Using everyday language way of describing this, GA is less "touchy-feely."

A final difference has to do with the kind of awareness or "consciousness" that develops in the two programs. In AA, one of the 12 Steps refers to restoring members to "sanity." In GA, the equivalent step statement refers to restoring members to "a normal way of thinking and living." While both groups subscribe to the disease model of addiction, GA focuses on gambling as the illness, while AA emphasizes an underlying illness of which alcohol consumption is merely the symptom. The goal of restoring "normality" has a significantly different meaning than the goal of restoring "sanity." Browne (1991) concluded that GA's adaptation of the AA program contributes to a transformation of the compulsive gambler by emphasizing a "secular, medically oriented path" rather than the "spiritually oriented path" presented in the AA program.

Based on participant observation research in Gamblers Anonymous, Livingston (1974) described the process of developing an attachment to and identification with GA as involving several stages. A crisis of some kind usually leads to initial attendance at a GA meeting. While newcomers may experience anxiety about discussing their gambling problems in front of strangers, they are relieved to learn that they are not alone. They find that others do not judge their behavior or ridicule them, since they have the same problems. Consequently, newcomers are able to be honest about their behavior and problems without being embarrassed. Gradually, they come to identify with other GA members because their experiences are so similar. Eventually, they internalize the GA concept of the nature of their problem and how they can deal with it.

Only a few researchers have attempted to evaluate GA's effectiveness. The research results suggest that GA is less effective than AA in achieving abstinence (Preston and Smith, 1975; Lesieur and Custer, 1984). One explanation for this has to do with how alcoholism and compulsive gambling are defined and how alcoholics and compulsive gamblers are "labeled."

Preston and Smith (1985) argued that both alcoholics and compulsive gamblers are seen by others and by themselves as "deviants." The AA and GA recovery programs attempt to "delabel" (eliminate the deviant label) and "relabel" (develop a new label that accounts for the behavior in a new way). In the case of AA, the alcoholic's behavior is relabeled as a physical illness over which the alcoholic has no control. The development of this "physical illness" label has occurred over a long period of time, and now its use is widespread. Labels with a culturally shared meaning (illness, disease) can be used to "understand" the problem. Although compulsive gambling is formally recognized as a "mental disorder" by psychiatrists, there is no evidence of physical illness or disease, so it cannot be labeled as such. Presumably, this difference in the ease and success with which compulsive gamblers can be relabeled accounts for at least some of the difference in the effectiveness of the AA and GA programs.

A study of first-time attenders of a GA meeting in Scotland sheds some light on why some people persist in attending GA meetings and others drop out. Both those who persist in attending and those who drop out indicated that they obtained useful information and advice and felt that they learned about their own problems by listening to others talk about theirs. However, those who dropped out were more likely to believe that they could become "controlled gamblers." Compared to long time members of GA and those newcomers who persisted in attending, dropouts also believed that they had not yet reached a "low" as extreme as that of other members. This suggests that the heaviest gamblers with the most severe and intense problem persist in attending, and those who compare themselves to others and conclude that their problems are not all that serious tend to drop out (Brown, 1986, 1987a, 1987b). Another British study of 232 GA attenders found that only 8 percent were not gambling after one year, and that after two years, 7 percent were totally abstinent from gambling (Steward and Brown, 1988).

While compulsive gambling counselors generally regard spousal involvement in treatment and in GamAnon as important, the impact of the spouse's involvement on the compulsive gambler's recovery is not clear. One small-scale study of the spouses of compulsive gamblers found that whether or not they participated in GamAnon was unrelated to the compulsive gambler's relapse (return to gambling) after beginning the recovery process (Zion, et al., 1991). It is altogether possible, of course, that GamAnon participation was beneficial for the spouse if not for the compulsive gambler.

Compulsive Gambling Treatment and Public Policy

Chapter 6 noted that public policy has concerned itself largely with issues of tax revenues and economic development. Little public policy attention has been devoted to the issue of gambling's downside—compulsive gambling. This section examines public and private sector initiatives to address the issue of compulsive gambling prevention and treatment.

The National Level

Currently, no national public policy regarding compulsive gambling exists. No federal agency or program has as its primary focus education about or research on compulsive gambling or its treatment. Federal involvement has been limited to support for research on the prevalence of compulsive gambling and the sporadic funding of treatment for compulsive gamblers in some Veterans Administration hospitals. The Americans with Disabilities Act specifically excludes compulsive gambling (while including other mental disorders), even though it is recognized as a mental disorder by the American Psychiatric Association. The issue of compulsive gambling also has not found its way onto the agendas of private foundations.

In 1976 the federal Commission on the Review of the National Policy toward Gambling acknowledged the existence of compulsive gambling. Twenty years later, Congress passed and the president signed the National Gambling Impact Study Commission Act of 1996. The nine member commission is charged with studying the economic and social impacts of gambling in the United States, including the impact of compulsive gambling on individuals and their families. The commission is expected to complete its work and issue its report, including recommendations, toward the end of 1999. What kinds of policies emerge from this effort remains to be seen.

Nationally, efforts to recognize compulsive gambling as a treatable disorder and have it identified as a high priority public policy issue have been centered in the National Council on Problem Gambling (NCPG). The NCPG and its twenty-nine state affiliates are private, nonprofit organizations that promote public education about compulsive gambling and the development of expertise in the treatment of compulsive gambling. The NCPG has developed counselor training and certification programs, and offers training through state affiliate councils. Counselor training and certification are also available through the American Academy of Health Care Providers in the Addictive Disorders, based in Massachusetts, and through the American Compulsive Gambling Counselor Certification Board, based in New Jersey.

NCPG and its state affiliates advocate public and gambling industry responsibility for the financing of education and research on compulsive gambling, and the establishment of counselor training programs and treatment centers. The NCPG and its affiliates are *not* antigambling. They are not advocates for or against the further legalization of gambling.

NCPG can appropriately be regarded as a "social movement." It was founded in 1972 in New York, and its early members included recovering compulsive gamblers, recovering alcoholics, counselors, and a variety of advocates for the recognition of compulsive gambling as a treatable disorder. In recent years its membership has grown to include psychiatrists, clinical psychologists, and a small number of academic and nonacademic psychologists, lawyers, economists, and sociologists, as well as members of the gambling industry. NCPG is not formally affiliated with Gamblers Anonymous, but many of its "recovering" members are also active in Gamblers Anonymous chapters. During its almost twenty-seven year history, the organization has clearly broadened its membership base.

NCPG began publishing the *Journal of Gambling Behavior* in 1985. In 1990, the journal's name was changed to the *Journal of Gambling Studies*, a change that coincided with its joint sponsorship by the NCPG and the Institute for the Study of Gambling and Commercial Gaming at the University of Nevada, Reno. Since 1987 the NCPG has held an annual National Conference on Gambling Behavior that draws participants from around the world.

The NCPG and its affiliates have become hybrid advocacy and professional organizations. While no states certify or license compulsive gambling counselors, the NCPG counselor training and certification programs serve as indicators of basic competence in the treatment of compulsive gambling. A good deal of effort both nationally and at the state level has been aimed at getting legislatures, state gaming commissions, and state departments of human services to provide funding for public education, toll-free telephone hot-lines, counselor training, and treatment programs.

In November 1993, the NCPG issued a position paper calling for a national policy on compulsive gambling (National Council on Problem Gambling, 1993). The report was sent to all members of Congress, federal cabinet officials, and the governors and attorneys general of all fifty states. The key recommendations in the NCPG's position paper include: the inclusion of compulsive gambling and substance abuse in a national health-care plan; a national survey to develop prevalence rates on compulsive gambling, to study the social impacts and costs and benefits of legalized gambling, and to assess the impact of compulsive gambling on at-risk populations (youth, the elderly, women, minorities, and the medically indigent); the development of policies to address compulsive gambling in the federal criminal justice system and among military personnel; and the inclusion of compulsive gamblers under the same protections afforded those with other disabilities. The NCPG was instrumental in developing support for the National Gambling Impact Study Commission Act of 1996.

An important national "private policy" initiative has developed within the gambling industry. Since the late 1980s, the Promus Corporation, which operates Harrah's Hotels and Casinos in Nevada and Atlantic City, as well as several riverboat casinos, has had a compulsive gambling education, intervention, and counseling program for its employees. It recently has been exploring ways of intervening with customers who exhibit signs of compulsive gambling and promoting the idea of "responsible gaming" within the gambling industry.

Another significant initiative has come from within the gambling industry. In 1996, the American Gaming Association (the gaming industry's national trade association) created the National Center for Responsible Gaming. Located in Kansas City, Missouri, the center's task is "to promote research and collect information on problem and underage gambling . . . and to . . . fund research; create prevention, intervention and treatment strategies; act as a national clearinghouse for research findings; and provide assistance to state and local governments to encourage responsible gaming practices" (American Gaming Association, 1997).

These gambling industry efforts are important because they represent an acknowledgement of the existence of compulsive gambling (industry spokespersons and the American Gaming Association use the term "problem gamer"). Substantial funding for these efforts has come from major casino gambling corporations. And these industry initiatives may get the attention of public officials who, with a few important exceptions, have failed to address the issue of compulsive gambling.

Despite these developments, there are other indications that concern about compulsive gambling is not widely shared throughout the gambling industry. Articles in *Gaming and Wagering Business* magazine (the industry's major trade publication) frequently lament the lack of attention that casinos pay to the issue of compulsive gambling (e.g., Palermo, 1998).

Some of the marketing practices of casinos are also at odds with the promotion of responsible gaming. Most casinos target frequent, heavy gamblers for special promotions and complimentary gifts (known as "comps") that include such things as free travel, rooms, meals, show tickets, and the like. A few casinos have also developed credit cards that people can use to accumulate points and bonuses redeemable at casino properties. They work in much the same way that credit card users can accumulate "frequent flyer" miles through the use of credit cards linked to airlines. Ironically, Harrah's, one of the prominent leaders in the "responsible gaming" movement has a card issued through VISA that accumulates points that can be redeemed at Harrah's casinos. Caesars also issues what could be characterized as a "frequent gambler's" credit card that earns bonus checks redeemable for chips at cashier cages in Caesars' casinos (Horovitz, 1997; Gwynne, 1997). Finally, the easy availability of machines that dispense instant cash through credit cards in casinos and the liberal use of "markers" (short-term, no interest loans to gamblers by casinos) seems inconsistent with the ostensible commitment to the promotion of responsible gaming.

The State Level

State level support for education, prevention, and treatment has been modest at best. As of 1996, twenty-one states were operating or had provided funding for programs dealing with some aspect of compulsive gambling. In 1996 states had allocated an estimated $13 million for education, research, and treatment. While that figure may appear large in an absolute sense, it is small compared with funding for other human service programs. For example, while Texas provides $2 million per year (mainly from lottery profits) for compulsive gambling, in fiscal year 1997 the state allocated $122 million for alcohol and drug abuse programs (Cox et al, 1997). The low priority given to compulsive gambling by state policies can be illustrated by a look at funding in New Jersey a few years ago. During the 1990-91 fiscal year, the state of New Jersey received $783 million in gambling revenues and spent $260,000 (0.03 percent) on compulsive gambling education and treatment programs.

When states do provide funding, the money typically comes from the revenues or profits from gambling enterprises that the state licenses, taxes, or operates. Funding is usually legislated on an annual or biennial basis, and its reduction or elimination is common. The unpredictability of funding makes planning and continuity of programs difficult. It also illustrates the low priority given to the issue of compulsive gambling.

State councils affiliated with the NCPG play an important advocacy role at the state and local levels. Their efforts include educating the public about compulsive gambling, serving as an informational resource for the media, operating toll-free hotlines that people in trouble with their gambling can call for referral to a Gamblers Anonymous chapter or a counselor, and training human service agency counselors in the diagnosis and treatment of compulsive gambling.

At the state level, several Native American tribal governments that operate casinos have provided financial support for the work of NCPG affiliated councils in their states. Especially noteworthy are the Mashantucket Pequots in Connecticut, the Oneidas in Wisconsin, and the Seminoles in Florida.

Other casino operators have supported compulsive gambling education, prevention, and treatment efforts to varying degrees at the state level. In Illinois and Missouri, riverboat casino trade associations have provided funding for compulsive gambling programs. In Colorado, Louisiana, and Mississippi, casino operators have given verbal support (Cox et al., 1997).

Summary

Treatment of compulsive gambling is neither a simple nor a standardized process. To be effective, treatment must deal with the gambler's financial and legal problems as well as his or her relationships with employers, debtors, spouse, and other family members.

Several treatment issues continue to be debated. One of these is whether the goal of treatment should be abstinence from gambling or dealing with the reasons for gambling once abstinence has been achieved. Another is whether it is possible for compulsive gamblers to become "controlled" gamblers.

The absence of an empirically validated model of the causes of compulsive gambling has made it impossible to develop a standardized treatment model. Examination of the effectiveness of different approaches to treatment suggests that effective treatment should include: avoidance of other gamblers and gambling situations; stress management; treatment for depression, if present; challenging illogical beliefs and expectations; marriage and family counseling, where relevant; developing responsible financial planning and budgeting skills; a restitution plan to deal with debts and past borrowing; developing nongambling leisure interests; dealing with other addictions; and attending Gamblers Anonymous meetings.

While broadly modeled after the Alcoholics Anonymous program, GA differs from AA in important ways. It places less emphasis on "spirituality," regards gambling as *the* problem, and focuses less on the underlying causes of the problem.

Public policy efforts to deal with compulsive gambling are minimal. They are virtually absent at the federal level, and only modest state initiatives have funded prevalence studies, public education, counselor training, and treatment programs. Within the gambling industry compulsive gambling has been acknowledged as an authentic problem, and there have been efforts to promote "responsible gaming." Yet, gambling industry marketing practices and the easy availability of cash through credit cards at casino properties and loans from casinos raise questions about these commitments.

The National Council on Problem Gambling and its state affiliates are the primary advocates for the recognition of compulsive gambling as a treatable disorder. They have also provided leadership in the development of public awareness about compulsive gambling and the creation of counselor training and certification programs.

Chapter 11

Looking to the Future

What does the future hold for gambling? This chapter looks at the way technology is likely to affect gambling and makes some projections about the future of the major, established forms of gambling.

Several issues involving the use of the Internet for gambling will be explored, including virtual casinos, lottery play, and sports betting. How much Internet gambling is there? The phenomenon is growing and changing so rapidly that it is difficult to be precise. As of early 1998, one estimate put the number of casino, lottery, and race/sports books at 120 (Haring, 1998).

Two additional topics that will be explored in this chapter are in-flight gambling (on airplanes) and at-home gambling via phone, cable television, and computer.

Welcome to the Virtual Casino

According to Christiansen/Cummings Associates, there were approximately twenty casino sites operating on the Internet in early 1997 (Sinclair, 1997). None of these sites was located in the United States. Most originated from islands in the Caribbean where casino gambling is legal. Typically, the sites offer slot machines and card games such as blackjack and video poker. To establish an account, players must give the casino/site operator a credit card number or deposit a check. Winnings are credited to the account, and losses are deducted from it.

A number of issues arise in these virtual casinos, including basic questions about the legality, regulation, and honesty of the games, the security of information transmitted, and the recourse of players in the case of disputes about winnings and losses.

Legal Issues

In the United States, the federal government has left the regulation of gambling to the states. State laws lack the jurisdiction to deal with the limitless boundaries of the Internet. As one commentator on the issue has put it, "There is nothing real or tangible in a virtual casino: no cards, no coins, no dealers, no people. And, to date, no regulation" (McKeag, 1997). However, one state, Nevada, has taken action to attempt to create a monopoly of sorts regarding Internet gambling. In July 1997, the governor of Nevada signed into law a bill that makes it *illegal* for Nevada residents to place bets on Internet facilities based outside the state of Nevada and *legal* for licensed race and sports books, off-track betting facilities, and casinos in Nevada to accept bets over the Internet. The complex legal issues involved in enforcing this law will take time to sort out. To make the situation even more complicated, at least two other states (Missouri and Pennsylvania) have laws that seem to make it illegal for an Internet operator to accept bets from their state's residents. In New York legislation has been passed that allows the New York Racing Association to accept bets via telephone from people in other states (Rose, 1997). How states where off-track betting is not legal treat the legality of calls originating in their states remains to be seen.

In early 1997, U.S. Senator Jon Kyl (Republican, Arizona) introduced Senate Bill 474, the Internet Prohibition Act of 1997. This bill would amend the Federal Wire Statute, which was intended to criminalize the transmission of mainly horse race results over telephone lines. SB 474 would criminalize placing or accepting a bet on the Internet, and would authorize the Federal Communications Commission to develop and enforce Internet regulations for companies that transmit foreign or domestic gambling information. The bill is significant because it attempts to give the federal government jurisdiction over communications coming into the United States from outside its borders.

While the legality of Americans gambling on the Internet through companies located outside the United States is an issue that needs to be addressed, a development closer to home is likely to be an issue much sooner. The Coeur D'Alene Tribe of Plummer, Idaho, established an Internet lottery Web site in January 1998 (Haring, 1998). The legal issues surrounding Internet gambling will be complicated by the special status of Native American tribes as "dependent sovereign nations" as well as the absence of state laws dealing with Internet gambling. Within a month of the opening of this lottery site, the attorneys general of thirty-five states asked the National Indian Gaming Commission to shut it down. In February 1998, a U.S. district court judge ruled that the State of Wisconsin could not sue the Coeur D'Alene Tribe because of its sovereign nation status, but it could sue the company (Unistar) operating the lottery for the tribe for offering its games to Wisconsin residents (*Kenosha News,* 1998).

Regulation

When gambling in a casino, there are two things that one wants to be sure of: that the games are honest and that if one wins one will be paid. Because there is no regulation of Internet gambling, one cannot be sure that these two conditions will be met.

In December 1996, the Internet Services Association, an interactive industry trade association, was formed. It created an Interactive Gaming Council, which takes the position that Internet gaming needs to be controlled and regulated and that regulation should come from within the industry. This position seems destined to conflict with the perspective that regulation should be done by an external, governmental body. Public policy in established gambling jurisdictions like Nevada and Atlantic City, as well as more recently established gambling venues, holds the view that self-regulation is no regulation at all. Whether regulation is located within or outside the Internet gambling industry, a major issue is likely to be how a U.S. based organization, private or public, can regulate an activity located outside the United States.

What If You Are
(or Think You Are) Ripped Off?

If an Internet gambler believes that credit card information has been used inappropriately, or that winnings and losses have been inaccurately recorded, what recourse is available? The answer is by no means clear, but it increasingly seems to be "none."

These questions have been considered by Jim Wortman, director of the University of Houston's Office of Gaming Education and Research. Wortman points out that if a win doesn't get credited to a gambler's account, it would not be possible to get help from the U.S. law enforcement agencies, since the casino operator is located outside the country. The gambler could sue the Internet casino company, but he or she would have to hire a lawyer in the country in which the Internet casino operates. Legal action could proceed only if that country has laws permitting the collection of gambling debts, and a favorable legal outcome would produce payment only if the casino operator actually has assets in the country in which the suit takes place (Connor, 1997).

Hazards also exist for Internet casino operators. The possibility of computer "hackers" accessing the site software is very real. Doing so would make it possible for the hacker to manipulate the outcome of games and the crediting and deducting of money to accounts (Connor, 1997).

The Virtual Lottery

Several state lotteries have informational Internet sites (Kentucky, Pennsylvania, Virginia) where people can check winning lottery numbers. The Virginia lottery, which has been operating its site since 1994, averages fifteen thousand "hits" per week. However, no U.S. state lottery is currently giving serious consideration to selling tickets or offering other forms of gambling on the Internet.

Internet lottery gambling is moving ahead in Europe. As of March 1997, three countries were operating Internet lotteries: Finland, Liechtenstein, and Gibraltar. Finland's site includes the opportunity to bet on sporting events as well as play lottery games. Lottery play and sports betting are limited to people within Finland. Gamblers around the world can play at the Liechtenstein and Gibraltar lottery sites (McQueen, 1997).

Gambling at these sites poses some of the same problems as gambling at virtual casinos, but players can be a bit less anxious, since these government operated lotteries are regulated and have readily identifiable "owners."

The Virtual Sports Book

Early in 1997, there were approximately sixty Internet sites offering to take bets on sporting events. While most of these Internet sports books were operating out of Caribbean countries, there were also sites originating from Australia and Austria. Again, many of the problems and issues that exist for virtual casinos also exist for virtual sports books.

The research firm of Christiansen/Cummings Associates estimates that there is a significant market for Internet sports betting in the United States. The market consists mainly of gamblers who currently bet on sporting events illegally through a bookie. While no one really knows how much money is bet this way, estimates range from $30 billion to $85 billion.

Sebastian Sinclair, a research analyst at Christiansen/Cummings, estimates that, given the expected growth in Internet users, the annual Internet sports handle could be as high as $760 million by the year 2000 (Sinclair, 1997). David Herschman, chief executive officer of the Internet gambling site Virtual Vegas, estimates that between $5 million and $10 million was bet via the Internet on the 1998 Super Bowl (cited in Haring, 1998).

In-Flight Gambling

The technology exists (or is currently under development) to turn the backs of airplane seats into terminals with a variety of gambling games. While U.S. airlines and gambling operators and suppliers have proposed in-flight gambling, American regulators and legislators have resisted dealing with the issue.

However, as with Internet lotteries, several European airlines are installing interactive terminals with a variety of games including conventional gambling games. They can be played through the use of credit cards. None of these airlines will be offering gambling games on flights to or from the United States in the foreseeable future. The reason for this is that, in 1994, Congress passed legislation banning gambling on international flights originating or ending in the United States. However, as foreign carriers install in-flight gambling devices on other flights, pressure is likely to mount to allow U.S. carriers to compete on a level playing field.

British Airways expected to have such a system operating on one of its four hundred seat 707s by the end of 1997 and plans to eventually offer a variety of gambling games on all of its 747s and 777s. Blackjack, roulette, and recorded horse races will be offered. Plans to install gambling devices are also moving ahead at Debonair Airways (a regional European carrier) and Swissair, which plans to have lotto, keno, and video slots on twenty-one of its planes. The Spanish carrier Oasis International Airlines, and PetrolAir, a Swiss carrier, also plan to install gambling devices on their planes. And by January 1998, Singapore Airlines expected to have blackjack, slots, and poker on fifty of its flights (Parets, 1996; Schoenstein, 1997).

Potential profits from in-flight gambling appear to be substantial. By one estimate, a four hundred seat plane could generate about $1 million in revenues per year. According to Russell Werdin, president of Intergame, a manufacturer of software for cashless machines (machines that would credit and debit credit card accounts), the potential gross revenue from in-flight gambling is about $2 billion per year (Schoenstein, 1997).

At-Home Gambling

Opportunities to gamble from home would be particularly attractive to people who cannot get to race tracks, casinos, or lottery ticket sales outlets because of physical limitations, age, inclement weather, or lack of transportation. The technology to create a number of at-home gambling options exists, but legal obstacles stand in the way of their implementation. In some

161

cases, legislation specifically prohibits certain forms of gambling. In other cases, legislation would be needed to authorize a lottery board or gaming commission to license or operate a particular kind of at-home gambling.

One solution would be to permit race tracks and OTBs to take bets over the phone. Telephone betting is legal in six states. As race tracks confront an increasingly competitive environment, the expansion of telephone betting could increase the racing handle and the taxes states receive, making tracks more viable. It would (technically) be a simple matter for tracks to have Internet Web sites that display the day's racing program and the odds on each race. Gamblers would simply place a bet by phone or at the Web site.

Another possibility is phone-in lottery ticket purchases. Once having established an account through the use of a credit card or cash deposit, lottery players could purchase tickets for a variety of lottery games by means of telephone menus or live operators.

Televised bingo games are another possibility. Bingo cards could be purchased in advance over the phone and faxed to the player. Or, they could be ordered via computer through e-mail or a Web site and printed by the player on a desktop printer.

Technology is also being developed to make television sets interactive, much like computers. At that point, the television set becomes a potential virtual casino, race track, OTB, bingo parlor, or lottery ticket sales outlet.

Other Issues

The racing segment of the gambling industry is unlikely to expand. With increasing competition from Native American reservation casinos and waterborne casinos, they will do well to hold their own. In an effort to survive, let alone be profitable, it is likely that tracks will generate proposals to add more off-track betting facilities, intertrack wagering, and casino games (slots, video poker, table games) to their racing facilities.

Lottery sales have slowed down in recent years. It is difficult to identify current developments that are likely to lead to a dramatic change in the relative position of lotteries within the gambling industry. While there will be variation between states, lottery advertising is likely to become more aggressive, and the development of new games (jackpots as well as instant or scratch-off games) is likely to become more frenzied.

Growth in the number of Native American tribes operating casinos has slowed in the late 1990s. It is not likely that many new tribes will enter the casino business in the early 2000s. In late 1997, members of the Navajo tribe in New Mexico, Arizona, and Utah voted down a proposal to open five casinos on their 17.5 million acre reservation. The vote was 54 percent for the proposal and 46 percent against (New View, 1998). Whether this is an indication of a new trend or an atypical event is difficult to tell.

Tribes already operating successful casinos will probably expand existing facilities, develop multiple locations on reservations, and seek to develop new properties in off-reservation locations. Since most reservation casinos are located in rural areas away from urban population centers, off-reservation developments, especially in or near urban areas, will bring casino gambling to potential customers rather than trying to attract customers to the reservations.

The expansion of land-based or waterborne gambling to new jurisdictions is difficult to predict. Because of referenda and legislative actions at the state level since 1995, there has been a slowdown in the expansion of these kinds of gambling venues. While states have turned down proposals for new gambling sites (especially riverboats), the approval of three casino licenses in Detroit stands out as an exception.

In the non-Native American casino industry, a kind of maturing is taking place. In the 1980s and 1990s, a substantial growth of new casino corporations took place, some of them relatively small, emerging in response to the expansion of riverboat gambling. In the early 2000s, a number of mergers and acquisitions are likely to result in a handful of major casino corporations gradually but surely coming to dominate the casino segment.

The traditional gambling venues of Nevada and Atlantic City are expected to continue to grow. The growth of Mississippi Gulf Coast casinos will make this area a serious gambling destination. It is difficult to identify any development that is likely to dramatically alter the focus on theme park destination resort growth in Las Vegas. While Atlantic City has not had theme parks, the early 2000s will see their emergence there as part of a strategy to make Atlantic City a destination resort and reduce its reliance on daytrippers as the primary customer base.

As Las Vegas becomes more Disneyesque, will Disney World (and possibly other entertainment resorts) become more Las Vegasesque? This is an intriguing question but not one that is easy to answer. The Disney Corporation is already in the gambling business. It operates a Caribbean cruise ship with a casino, suggesting that "Disney" and "gambling" are not completely incompatible. Could "Casino Land" stand alongside Fantasy Land, Adventure Land, and Tomorrow Land in the Magic Kingdom in the future? It's not unthinkable!

Summary

The emergence and growth of the Internet has provided new possibilities and opportunities for gambling. Internet sites offering casino games, lottery play, and sports/race books already exist and will continue to become more numerous despite questions about their legality and a host of regulatory issues.

In-flight gambling on airplanes exists and will expand. Technological developments have expanded opportunities for in-home gambling via telephone, cable television, and computers. As with Internet gambling, legal issues and prohibitions currently stand in the way of their implementation.

As the casino gambling industry matures, consolidations and mergers are likely to occur. Theme park development will continue in Las Vegas and elsewhere, lotteries are expected to remain stable, and the racing segment will struggle with competition from land-based and waterborne casino developments.

References

Chapter 1

American Psychiatric Association. 1994. *Diagnostic and Statistical Manual of Mental Disorders.* 4th ed. Washington, DC: APA.

Ashton, John. 1968. *A History of Gambling in England.* Detroit, MI: Singing Tree Press.

Bernstein, Peter L. 1996. *Against the Gods: The Remarkable Story of Risk.* New York: Wiley.

Campbell, Colin S., and John Lowman. 1989. *Gambling in Canada: Golden Goose or Trojan Horse?* Burnaby, British Columbia: Simon Fraser University.

Clotfelter, Charles T., and Philip J. Cook. 1989. *Selling Hope: State Lotteries in America.* Cambridge: Harvard University Press.

Custer, Robert, and Harry Milt. 1985. *When Luck Runs Out: Help for Compulsive Gamblers and Their Families.* New York: Facts on File.

Downes, D.M. 1976. *Gambling, Work, and Leisure: A Study across Three Areas.* London: Routledge and Kegan Paul.

Drake, St. Clair, and Horace Cayton. 1945. *Black Metropolis.* New York: Harcourt, Brace and World.

Elliott, Russell R. 1973. *History of Nevada.* Lincoln: University of Nebraska Press.

Estes, Ken. 1990. *Deadly Odds: The Compulsion to Gamble.* Newport, RI: Edgehill.

Ezell, John S. 1960. *Fortune's Merry Wheel: The Lottery in America.* Cambridge, MA: Harvard University Press.

Findlay, John M. 1986. *People of Chance: Gambling in American Society from Jamestown to Las Vegas.* New York: Oxford University Press.

Frazier, E. Franklin. 1957. *Black Bourgeoisie: The Rise of a New Middle Class in the United States.* Glencoe, IL: Free Press.

Freud, Sigmund. 1961. "Dostoevsky and Parricide." In James Strachey, ed., *The Complete Works of Sigmund Freud.* Vol. 21. London: Hogarth Press.

Geisler, Norman L. 1990. *Gambling: A Bad Bet.* Old Tappan, NJ: Power Books.

Goodman, Robert. 1995. *The Luck Business: The Devastating Consequences and Broken Promises of America's Gambling Explosion.* New York: Free Press.

Hayano, David M. 1982. *Poker Faces.* Berkeley: University of California Press.

Herman, Robert. 1967. "Gambling as Work: A Sociological Study of the Racetrack." In Robert Herman, ed., *Gambling,* pp. 87–106. New York: Harper and Row.

Lears, Jackson. 1995. "Playing with Money." *Wilson Quarterly,* Autumn, pp. 6–23.

Lesieur, Henry R., and Sheila B. Blume. 1987. "The South Oaks Gambling Screen (the SOGS): A New Instrument for the Identification of Pathological Gamblers." *American Journal of Psychiatry,* 144: 1184–1188.

Longstreet, Stephen. 1977. *Win or Lose: A Social History of Gambling in America.* New York: Bobbs-Merrill.

Martinez, Thomas M., and Robert La Franchi. 1969. "Why People Play Poker." *Transaction,* 6: 32–52.

Messick, Hank, and Burt Goldblatt. 1976. *The Only Game in Town: An Illustrated History of Gambling.* New York: Crowell.

Moody, Gordon. 1990. *Quit Compulsive Gambling.* Wellingborough, England: Thorsons Publishing Group.

Newman, Otto. 1972. "The Sociology of the Betting Shop." *British Journal of Sociology,* 19: 17–33.

Oldman, David. 1974. "Chance and Skill: A Study of Roulette." *Sociology,* 8: 407–426.

Oldman, David. 1978. "Compulsive Gamblers." *Sociological Review,* 26 (May) 349–370

Reid, Ed, and Ovid Demaris. 1963. *The Green Felt Jungle.* New York: Trident Press.

Rosecrance, John. 1985a. "Compulsive Gambling and the Medicalization of Deviance." *Social Problems,* 32 (February): 275–284

Rosecrance, John. 1985b. *The Degenerates of Lake Tahoe: A Study of Persistence in the Social World of Horse Race Gambling.* New York: Peter Lang.

Rosten, Leo. 1941. *Hollywood: The Movie Colony, The Movie Makers.* New York: Harcourt, Brace, and World.

Scott, Marvin B. 1968. *The Racing Game.* Chicago: Aldine.

Skolnick, Jerome H. 1978. *House of Cards: The Legalization and Control of Casino Gambling.* Boston: Little, Brown.

Tec, Nechama. 1964. *Gambling in Sweden.* Totowa, NJ: Bedminster.

Turner, Wallace. 1965. *Gambler's Money: The New Force in American Life.* Boston: Houghton Mifflin.

Wagner, Walter. 1972. *To Gamble or Not to Gamble.* New York: World.

Waller, Adrian. 1974. *The Gamblers.* Toronto: Clarke, Irwin.

Whyte, William Foote. 1943. *Street Corner Society.* Chicago: University of Chicago Press.

Zola, Irving Kenneth. 1963. "Observations on Gambling in a Lower-Class Setting." *Social Problems,* 10 (Spring):353–361.

Chapter 2

American Psychiatric Association. 1994. *Diagnostic and Statistical Manual of Mental Disorders.* 4th ed. Washington, DC: APA.

Clinard, Marshall B. 1957. *Sociology of Deviant Behavior.* New York: Rinehart.

Clotfelter, Charles T. and Philip J. Cook. 1989. *State Lotteries in America.* Cambridge, MA: Harvard University Press.

Devereux, Edward C. 1949. "Gambling and Social Structure: A Sociological Study of Lotteries and Horse Racing in Contemporary America." Ph. D. diss., Harvard University, Cambridge, MA.

Downes, D. M. 1976. *Gambling, Work, and Leisure: A Study across Three Areas.* London: Routledge and Kegan Paul.

Drake, St. Clair, and Horace Cayton. 1945. *Black Metropolis.* New York: Harcourt, Brace, and World.

Frazier, E. Franklin. 1957. *Black Bourgeoisie: The Rise of a New Middle Class in the United States.* Glencoe, IL: Free Press.

Geis, Gilbert. 1972. *Not the Law's Business?* Washington, DC: U.S. Government Printing Office.

Goffman, Erving. 1961. *Encounters.* Indianapolis, IN: Bobbs-Merrill.

Goffman, Erving. 1967. *Interaction Ritual.* New York: Anchor Books.

Goode, Erich. 1994. *Deviant Behavior.* 4th ed. Englewood Cliffs, NJ: Prentice-Hall.

Hayano, David M. 1982. *Poker Faces.* Berkeley: University of California Press.

Herman, Robert. 1967. "Gambling at Work: A Sociological Study of the Racetrack." In Robert Herman, ed., *Gambling.* New York: Harper and Row. pp. 87–106.

Kaplan, H. Roy. 1979. "The Convergence of Work, Sport, and Gambling in America." *The Annals.* 445 (September): 24–38.

Kitano, Harry H. L. 1976. *Japanese Americans: The Evolution of a Subculture.* Englewood Cliffs, NJ: Prentice-Hall.

Leong, Gor Yun. 1936. *Chinatown Inside Out.* New York: Barrows Mussey.

Lyman, Stanform M. 1974. *Chinese Americans.* New York: Random House.

Martinez, Thomas M., and Robert La Franchi. 1969. "Why People Play Poker." *Transaction.* 6:32–52.

Newman, Otto. 1968. "The Sociology of the Betting Shop." *British Journal of Sociology.* 19:17–33.

Oldman, David. 1974. "Chance and Skill: A Study of Roulette." *Sociology.* 8: 407–426

Oldman, David. 1978. "Compulsive Gamblers." *Sociological Review.* 26: 349–370.

Pfohl. Stephen. 1994. *Images of Deviance and Social Control: A Sociological History.* 2nd ed. New York: McGraw-Hill.

Rosecrance, John. 1985. *The Degenerates of Lake Tahoe: A Study of Persistence in the Social World of Horse Race Gambling.* New York: Peter Lang.

Scott, Marvin B. 1968. *The Racing Game.* Chicago: Aldine.

Skolnick, Jerome H. 1978. *House of Cards: The Legalization and Control of Casino Gambling.* Boston: Little, Brown.

Thio, Alex. 1988. *Deviant Behavior.* 3rd ed. New York: HarperCollins.

Trotter, Joe William, Jr. 1985. *Black Milwaukee: The Making of an Industrial Proletariat, 1915-1945.* Urbana: University of Illinois Press.

Veblen, Thorstein. 1953. *The Theory of the Leisure Class.* New York: Mentor Books.

Ward, David A., et al. 1994. *Social Deviance: Being, Behaving, and Branding.* Boston: Allyn and Bacon.

Whyte, William Foote. 1943. *Street Corner Society.* Chicago: University of Chicago Press.

Zola, Irving Kenneth. 1963. "Observations on Gambling in a Lower-Class Setting." *Social Problems,* 10 (Spring): 353–361

Chapter 3

Campbell, Colin S. and Garry J. Smith. 1998. "Canadian Gambling: Trends and Public Policy Issues." *The Annals,* 556 (March): 22–35.

DeJuana, Carlos A. 1997. "Mexico: Is the Game Over?" *Gaming and Wagering Business,* 18, no. 11 (November): S6.

Dombrink, John, and William N. Thompson. 1990. *The Last Resort: Success and Failure in Campaigns for Casinos.* Reno: University of Nevada Press.

Doocey, Paul. 1997a. "Casino Legislation Likely on Hold until September." *Gaming and Wagering Business,* 18, no. 1 (January): 4.

Doocey, Paul. 1997b. "Fasten Your Seatbelts." *Gaming and Wagering Business,* 18, no. 6 (June): S7.

Ezell, John S. 1960. *Fortune's Merry Wheel: The Lottery in America.* Cambridge, MA: Harvard University Press.

Fabian, Ann. 1990. *Card Sharps, Dream Books, and Bucket Shops: Gambling in Nineteenth-Century America.* Ithaca, NY: Cornell University Press.

Findlay, John M. 1986. *People of Chance: Gambling in American Society from Jamestown to Las Vegas.* New York: Oxford University Press.

Gaming and Wagering Business. 1997a. "Casino Niagara Opening Is a Hit." *Gaming and Wagering Business,* 18, no. 3 (March): 22.

Gaming and Wagering Business. 1997b. "1997 Australia and New Zealand Gambling Report." *Gaming and Wagering Business,* 18, no. 3 (March): S4–S22.

Haller, Mark H. 1979. "The Changing Structure of American Gambling in the Twentieth Century." *Journal of Social Issues,* 35, no. 3: 87–114.

Johnson, David R. 1977. "A Sinful Business: Origins of Gambling Syndicates in the United States, 1840-1887." In David Bayley, ed., *Police and Society.* Beverly Hills, CA: Sage.

Joyce, Kathleen M. 1979. "Public Opinion and the Politics of Gambling." *Journal of Social Issues,* 35, no. 3: 144-165.

McQueen, Patricia A. 1996a. "Passing the Century Mark." *Gaming and Wagering Business,* 17, no. 5 (May): 45.

McQueen, Patricia A. 1996b. "World Gaming at a Glance." *Gaming and Wagering Business,* 17, no. 10 (October): 80–84.

North American Gaming Report. 1996. *Gaming and Wagering Business,* 17, no. 7 (July): S32–S38.

North American Gaming Report. 1997. *Gaming and Wagering Business,* 18, no. 7 (July): S32–S38.

Rose, I. Nelson. 1986. *Gambling and the Law.* Los Angeles, CA: Gambling Times.

Rose, I. Nelson, 1995. "Gambling and the Law: Endless Fields of Dreams." *Journal of Gambling Studies,* 11 (Spring): 15–33.

Rosecrance, John. 1988. *Gambling Without Guilt.* Pacific Grove, CA: Brooks/Cole.

Sasuly, Richard. 1982. *Bookies and Bettors: Two Hundred Years of Gambling.* New York: Holt, Rinehart and Winston.

Sullivan, G. 1972. *By Chance a Winner.* New York: Dodd, Mead.

Thompson, William N. 1998. "Casinos de Juegos del Mundo: A Survey of World Gambling." *The Annals,* 556 (March): 11–21.

Weinstein, D., and L. Deitch. 1974. *The Impact of Legalized Gambling: The Socioeconomic Consequences of Lotteries and Off-Track Betting.* New York: Praeger.

Chapter 4

Christiansen, Eugene M. 1993. "Industry Rebounds with 8.4% Handle Gain." *Gaming and Wagering Business,* 14, no. 7 (August): 12–35.

Christiansen, Eugene M. 1997. "1996 Gross Annual Wager." *Gaming and Wagering Business,* 17, no. 8: 20.

Clotfelter, Charles T., and Philip J. Cook. 1989. *Selling Hope: State Lotteries in America.* Cambridge, MA: Harvard University Press.

Commission on the Review of the National Policy Toward Gambling. 1976. *Gambling in America.* Washington, DC: U.S. Government Printing Office.

Gaming and Wagering Business. 1997. "North American Gaming Report, 1997." *Gaming and Wagering Business,* 18, no. 7 (July): S19–S22.

McQueen, Patricia A. 1996. "North American Gaming at a Glance." *Gaming and Wagering Business,* 17, no. 9 (September): 52–56.

Chapter 5

American Psychiatric Association. 1994. *Diagnostic and Statistical Manual of Mental Disorders.* 4th ed. Washington, DC: APA.

Anders, Gary C. 1996. "Native American Casino Gambling in Arizona: A Case Study of the Fort McDowell Reservation." *Journal of Gambling Studies,* 12 (Fall): 253–267.

Andersen, Arthur. 1996. *Economic Impacts of Casino Gaming in the United States. Vol. 1: Macro Study.* Washington, DC: American Gaming Association.

Andersen, Arthur. 1997. *Economic Impacts of Casino Gaming in the United States. Vol. 2: Micro Study.* Washington, DC: American Gaming Association.

Charlier, Marj. 1992. "The Payoff: Casino Gambling Saves Three Colorado Towns But the Price Is High." *Wall Street Journal,* September 23, p. A5.

Coopers and Lybrand. 1997. *Gaming Industry Employee Impact Survey.* Las Vegas, NV: Coopers and Lybrand.

Evans Group, The. 1996. *A Study of the Economic Impact of the Gaming Industry Through 2005.* N.p.: Evans Group.

Goodman, Robert. 1995. *The Luck Business: The Devastating Consequences and Broken Promises of America's Gambling Explosion.* New York: Free Press.

Grinol, Earl L. 1994a. "Bluff or Winning Hand? Riverboat Gambling and Regional Employment and Unemployment." *Illinois Business Review,* Spring, pp. 8–11.

Grinol, Earl L. 1994b. Oral testimony before the Committee on Small Business, U.S. House of Representatives, September 21.

Harrah's. 1997. "Harrah's Employees Have Major Impact on Local Economies." News Release, Memphis, TN, February 18.

KPMG Peat Marwick. 1992. "Economic Benefits of Tribal Gaming in Minnesota." Minneapolis, MN, March.

McQueen, Patricia A. 1997. "Performance Barometers." *Gaming and Wagering Business,* 18, no. 4 (April): 30–43.

Midwest Hospitality Advisors. 1992. "Impact of Native American Gaming in the State of Minnesota." Minneapolis, MN: Midwest Hospitality Advisors.

Murray, James M. 1993. "The Economic Benefits of American Indian Gaming Facilities in Wisconsin." Green Bay: University of Wisconsin— Cooperative Extension.

O'Driscoll, Patrick. 1997. "Gambling Gulch Is Both Bonanza and Battleground." *USA Today,* October 27, pp. 17A–18A.

Plume, Janet. 1994. "Little Las Vegas Sprouting in Tunica." *Casino Journal,* September, pp. 79–81.

Smith, Wes. 1994. "A Winning Hand: A Poor Delta Town Floats High on Gambling's Inflating Tide." *Chicago Tribune,* June 30, Sect. 5, pp. 1, 11.

SMR Research Corp. 1997. *The Personal Bankruptcy Crisis, 1997.* Hackettstown, NJ: SMR Research Corp.

Stedham, Yvonne, and Merwin C. Mitchell. 1996. "Voluntary Turnover among Non-Supervisory Casino Employees." *Journal of Gambling Studies,* 12 (Fall): 269–290.

Stokowski, Patricia A. 1992. "The Colorado Gambling Boom: An Experiment in Rural Community Development." *Small Town,* May-June, pp. 12–19.

Stokowski, Patricia A. 1996. *Riches and Regrets: Betting on Gambling in Two Colorado Mountain Towns.* Niwot, CO: University Press of Colorado.

Thompson, William, et al. 1995. *The Economic Impact of Native American Gaming in Wisconsin.* Milwaukee, WI: Wisconsin Policy Research Institute.

Thompson, William N., and Ricardo C. Gazel. 1996. *The Monetary Impacts of Riverboat Casino Gambling in Illinois.* Chicago: Better Government Association.

University Associates. 1992. Economic Impact of Michigan's Native American Gaming Enterprises. Lansing, MI: University Associates.

Wisconsin Legislative Reference Bureau. 1995. *State of Wisconsin 1995-1996 Blue Book.* Madison, WI: Department of Administration.

Chapter 6

Clotfelter, Charles T., and Philip J. Cook. 1989. *Selling Hope: State Lotteries in America.* Cambridge, MA: Harvard University Press.

Christiansen, Eugene Martin, et al. 1996. "1995 Gross Annual Wager," *Gaming and Wagering Business,* 17, no. 8 (August): 66.

Dombrink, John, and William N. Thompson. 1990. *The Last Resort: Success and Failure in Campaigns for Casinos.* Reno: University of Nevada Press.

Doocey, Paul. 1996. "Gaming Scores in Michigan and Arizona." *Gaming and Wagering Business,* 17 (December): 1, 4.

Eadington, William R. 1995. "Gambling: Philosophy and Policy." *Journal of Gambling Studies,* 11 (Spring): 9–13.

Findlay, John M. 1986. *People of Chance.* New York: Oxford University Press.

Governor's Blue Ribbon Task Force on Gambling. 1992. *Report of the Task Force.* Madison, WI, January 13.

Kenosha News. 1997. "Tribal Casinos Compared to Other Gambling Meccas." *Kenosha News,* June 13, p. A7.

Milwaukee Journal. 1993. "Police Crack Down on Video Gambling." *Milwaukee Journal,* June 6.

Milwaukee Journal. 1992. "State Far from Ready to Allow Track Casinos." *Milwaukee Journal,* October 28, p. A17.

Piliavin, Irving, and Josh Rossol. 1995. *Gambling in Wisconsin: A Third Look at Wisconsin Lottery Play.* Special Report 63. Madison, WI: Institute for Research on Poverty, University of Wisconsin.

Racine Journal Times. 1993a. "State Bishops Back Anti-Gambling Measure." *Racine Journal Times,* March 4, p. 3C.

Racine Journal Times. 1993b. "Churches, Tribes Planning Opposite Campaigns on Gambling Amendment." *Racine Journal Times,* March 3, p. 4B.

Rose, I. Nelson. 1995. "Gambling and the Law: Endless Fields of Dreams." *Journal of Gambling Studies,* 11 (Spring): 15–33.

Thompson, William N., and Ricardo Gazel. 1995. "The Last Resort Revisited: A Comment on Changes in America." *Journal of Gambling Studies,* 11 (Winter): 373–378.

Chapter 7

Ader, Jason, and Clayton Moran. 1993. *National Gaming Review.* N.p.: Smith, Barney, Shearson.

Chicago Tribune. 1992. "Daley Embraces $2 Billion Casino Plan: Proposal Leaves Mayor's Foes, Allies Dumbstruck." *Chicago Tribune,* March 25, pp. 1, 16.

Circus Enterprises. 1992. *Annual Report.* Las Vegas, NV: Circus Enterprises, Inc.

Dean Witter. 1992. "The Gaming Industry: Las Vegas Update." *Equity Research Report,* No. 1783, October 21. N.p.: Dean Witter.

Doocey, Paul. 1994a. "Kentucky Tracks Eye Casino Projects." *Gaming and Wagering Business,* 15, no. 2: 1, 40.

Doocey, Paul 1994b. "Will OTB Be DOA?" *Gaming and Wagering Business,* 15, no. 2: 18–21.

Gaming and Wagering Business. 1993a. "Nov. 3 Gaming-Related Ballot Scoreboard." *Gaming and Wagering Business,* 15, no. 12: 38.

Gaming and Wagering Business. 1993b. "What to Look For as This Year in Gaming Unfurls." *Gaming and Wagering Business,* 15, no. 1: 1, 29-30.

Gaming and Wagering Business. 1997. "Mall Inks Casino Tenant." *Gaming and Wagering Business*, 18, no. 4: 10.

Grossman, Cathy Lynn. 1993. "Las Vegas Deals New Hand of Family Fun." *USA Today,* August 10, p. 4D.

Pierce, Neal. 1992. "Gambling: Clean Family Fun and 'Easy' Money." *Liberal Opinion,* December 21.

Rosecrance, John. 1988. *Gambling Without Guilt.* Pacific Grove, CA: Brooks/Cole.

Skolnick, Jerome H. 1978. *House of Cards: The Legalization and Control of Casino Gambling.* Boston: Little, Brown.

Vogel, Jennifer, ed. 1997. *Crapped Out.* Monroe, ME: Common Courage Press.

Chapter 8

Abbott, Douglas A., and Sheran L. Cramer. 1993. "Gambling Attittudes and Participation: A Midwestern Survey." *Journal of Gambling Studies,* 9 (Fall): 247–263.

Casino Journal. 1994. "Bet on It!" *Casino Journal,* September.

Doocey, Paul. 1996. "The Case for Legal Sports Betting." *Gaming and Wagering Business,* 17, no. 4 (April): 1, 40–43.

Gallup, George, Jr. 1989. *The Gallup Report,* 285 (June), pp. 38-39.

Gallup Organization. 1993. *New Jersey Residents' Attitudes and Behavior Regarding Gambling.* Princeton, NJ: Gallup Organization, Inc.

Gaming and Wagering Business. 1994. "North American Gaming Report, 1994." Supplement. *Gaming and Wagering Business,* July.

Gray, Jack. 1991. *Wisconsin Gaming Survey: Awareness, Activity and Opinion.* N.p.: Diversified Communications Services.

Harrah's. 1996. *Harrah's Survey of Casino Entertainment.* Memphis, TN: N.p.

Harrah's. 1997. *Harrah's Survey of Casino Entertainment.* Memphis, TN: N.p.

Harrah's Casino Hotels. 1994. *The Harrah's Survey of U.S. Casino Gaming Entertainment.* Memphis, TN: Gaming Division of the Promus Companies, Inc.

Harshbarger, S. 1994. *Report on the Sale of Lottery Tickets to Minors in Massachusetts.* Boston: Attorney General, Commonwealth of Massachusetts.

Lefebvre, Joan E., and Alice F. Kempen. 1995. *Gambling Participation Survey Report.* Eagle River: University of Wisconsin Extension.

Lesieur, Henry R. 1988. "The Female Pathological Gambler." In William R. Eadington, ed., *Gambling Research: Proceedings of the 7th International Conference on Gambling and Risk Taking.* Reno: Bureau of Business and Economic Research, University of Nevada, Reno.

Lindgren, H. Elaine, et al. 1987. "The Impact of Gender on Gambling Attitudes and Behavior." *Journal of Gambling Behavior,* 3 (Fall): 155–167.

McAneny, Leslie. 1992. "Gambling Behavior." *The Gallup Poll Monthly,* 327 (December): 5–11.

McGraw, Dan. 1997. "The National Bet." *U.S. News and World Report,* April 7, pp. 50–55.

Pavalko, Ronald M. and Alan E. Bayer. 1994. "Gambling Behavior and Attitudes Toward Gambling in Virginia." Paper presented at the Annual Meeting of the American Sociological Association, Los Angeles, CA, August.

Penaloza, Linda J., ed. 1997. "Majority of Wisconsinites Oppose Abolishing the State Lottery." *Wisconsin Opinions,* 6 (September).

Piliavin, Irving, and Josh Rossol. 1995. *Gambling in Wisconsin: A Third Look at Wisconsin Lottery Play.* Special Report 63. Madison: Institute for Research on Poverty, University of Wisconsin—Madison.

Radecki, Thomas E. 1994. "The Sales of Lottery Tickets to Minors in Illinois." *Journal of Gambling Studies,* 10 (Fall): 213–218.

Radecki, Thomas E. 1995. "The Sales of Lottery Tickets to Minors." Paper presented at the National Conference on Gambling, Crime, and Gaming Enforcement, Illinois State University, Normal, IL, April.

Roberts, Glenn. 1996. *Family and Consumer Sciences Poll: An Iowa Survey of Gambling Attitudes and Participation.* Des Moines, IA: Glen Roberts Research Group.

Saad, Lydia. 1992. "Gambling Attitudes." *The Gallup Poll Monthly,* 372 (December): 2–4.

St. Cloud State University. N.d. *Gambling in Minnesota.* St. Cloud, MN: Survey Research Center.

Thompson, William N., et al. 1993. "Not in My Backyard: Las Vegas Residents Protest Casinos." *Journal of Gambling Studies,* 9 (Spring): 47–62.

Townsend, Jay and Dick Dresner. 1992. *Public Attitudes Toward Expansion of Gambling in Wisconsin.* San Diego, CA: Dresner, Sykes, Jordan, and Townsend, Inc.

Volberg, Rachel A. 1993. *Gambling and Compulsive Gambling in Washington State.* Albany, NY: Gemini Research.

Volberg, Rachel A. 1994. *Gambling and Problem Gambling in South Dakota: A Follow-Up Survey.* Roaring Springs, PA: Gemini Research.

Volberg, Rachel A. 1995. *Gambling and Problem Gambling in Iowa: A Replication Survey.* Roaring Springs, PA: Gemini Research.

Volberg, Rachel A. 1996. *Gambling and Problem Gambling in New York: A 10-Year Replication Survey, 1986 to 1996.* Roaring Springs, PA: Gemini Research.

Wallisch, Lynn S. 1993. *Gambling in Texas: 1992 Texas Survey of Adult Gambling Behavior.* Austin: Texas Commission on Alcohol and Drug Abuse.

Wallisch, Lynn S. 1996. *Gambling in Texas: 1995 Surveys of Adult and Adolescent Gambling Behavior.* Austin: Texas Commission on Alcohol and Drug Abuse.

Zimmerman, S. 1996. "Kids Buy Into Lottery." *Chicago Sun-Times,* September 1, pp. 1-2.

Chapter 9

Abbott, Max W., and Rachel A. Volberg. 1996. "The New Zealand National Survey of Problem and Pathological Gambling." *Journal of Gambling Studies,* 12 (Summer): 143–160.

Ahrons, S.J. 1989. "A Comparison of the Family Environments and Psychological Distress of Married Pathological Gamblers, Alcoholics, Psychiatric Patients and Their Spouses with Normal Controls." Ph.D. diss., University of Maryland, College Park.

American Psychiatric Association. 1994. *Diagnostic and Statistical Manual of Mental Disorders.* 4th ed., Washington, DC: American Psychiatric Association.

Arcuri, A.F., et al. 1985. "Shaping Adolescent Gambling Behavior." *Adolescence,* 20: 935–938.

Becona, Elisardo. 1996. "Prevalence Surveys of Problem and Pathological Gambling in Europe: The Cases of Germany, Holland, and Spain." *Journal of Gambling Studies,* 12 (Summer): 179–192.

Bergler, Edmund. 1957. *The Psychology of Gambling.* New York: Hill and Wang.

Blackman, S. et al. 1986. "Treatment of Gamblers." *Hospital and Community Psychiatry,* 37: 404.

Blaszczynski, Alex and Neil McConaghy. 1989. "The Medical Model of Pathological Gambling: Current Shortcomings." *Journal of Gambling Behavior,* 5 (Spring): 42–52.

Blaszczynski, Alex and Neil McConaghy. 1994. "Criminal Offenses in Gamblers Anonymous and Hospital Treated Pathological Gamblers." *Journal of Gambling Studies,* 10 (Summer): 99–127.

Blume, Sheila B. 1987. "Compulsive Gambling and the Medical Model." *Journal of Gambling Behavior,* 3 (Winter): 237–247.

Blume, Sheila B. 1994. "Pathological Gambling and Switching Addictions: Report of a Case." *Journal of Gambling Studies,* 10 (Spring): 87–96.

Ciarrocchi, Joseph W., et al. 1991. "Personality Dimensions of Male Pathological Gamblers, Alcoholics, and Dually Addicted Gamblers." *Journal of Gambling Studies,* 7 (Summer): 133–141.

Ciarrocchi, Joseph W., and Ann Hohnmann. 1989. "The Family Environment of Married Male Pathological Gamblers, Alcoholics, and Dually Addicted Gamblers." *Journal of Gambling Behavior,* 5 (Winter): 283–291.

Council on Compulsive Gambling of New Jersey. 1991. "1-800 Hotline Statistics for 1990." *The Connection,* Spring, p. 9.

Cox, Sue, et al. 1997. "Problem and Pathological Gambling in America: The National Picture." Columbia, MD: National Council on Problem Gambling.

Custer, Robert, and Harry Milt. 1985. *When Luck Runs Out: Help for Compulsive Gamblers and Their Families.* New York: Facts on File Publications.

Dickerson, Mark. 1987. "The Future of Gambling Research—Learning from the Lessons of Alcoholism." *Journal of Gambling Studies,* 3 (Winter): 248–256.

Dickerson, Mark G. et al. 1996. "Estimating the Extent and Degree of Gambling Related Problems in the Australian Population: A National Survey." *Journal of Gambling Studies,* 12 (Summer): 161 –178.

Emerson, Michael O., and Laundergan, J. Clark. 1996. "Gambling and Problem Gambling among Adult Minnesotans: Changes 1990 to 1994." *Journal of Gambling Studies,* 12 (Fall): 291–304.

Epstein, Eileen A. 1992. "Family Functioning in the Families of Compulsive Gamblers." Ph. D. diss., New York University, New York.

Frank, Michael L., et al. 1991. "Suicidal Behavior among Members of Gamblers Anonymous." *Journal of Gambling Studies,* 7 (Fall): 249–253.

Freud, Sigmund. 1961. "Dostoevsky and Parricide." In James Strachey, ed., *The Complete Works of Sigmund Freud.* Vol. 21. London: Hogarth Press.

Graham, John R., and Beverly H. Lowenfeld. 1986. "Personality Dimensions of the Pathological Gambler." *Journal of Gambling Behavior,* 2 (Summer): 58–66.

Greenson, R. 1947. "On Gambling." *American Imago,* 4: 61–67.

Hunter, J., and A. Brunner. 1928. "The Emotional Outlets of Gamblers." *Journal of Abnormal and Social Psychology,* 23: 38-39.

Jacobs, Durand F. 1989a. "A General Theory of Addictions: Rationale for and Evidence Supporting a New Approach for Understanding and Treating Addictive Behaviors." In Howard J. Schaffer et al., *Compulsive Gambling: Theory, Research, and Practice,* pp. 35-64. Lexington, MA: Lexington Books.

Jacobs, Durand F. 1989b. "Illegal and Undocumented: A Review of Teenage Gamblers in America." In Howard J. Schaffer, et al., *Compulsive Gambling: Theory, Research, and Practice.* pp. 249-292. Lexington, MA: Lexington Books.

Jacobs, Durand F., et al. 1989c. "Children of Compulsive Gamblers." *Journal of Gambling Behavior,* 5 (Winter): 261–268.

Kallick, M., et al. 1979. *A Survey of American Gambling Attitudes and Behavior.* Research Report Series. Survey Research Center, Institute for Social Research. Ann Arbor: University of Michigan Press.

Ladouceur, Robert. 1996. "The Prevalence of Pathological Gambling in Canada." *Journal of Gambling Studies,* 12 (Summer): 129–142.

Ladouceur, Robert, et al. 1994. "Social Cost of Compulsive Gambling." *Journal of Gambling Studies,* 10 (Winter): 399–409.

Lesieur, Henry R. 1984. *The Chase: Career of the Compulsive Gambler.* Rochester, VT: Schenkman Books.

Lesieur, Henry R. 1988. "The Female Pathological Gambler." In W.R. Eadington, ed., *Gambling Research: Proceedings of the Seventh International Conference on Gambling and Risk Taking.* Reno: Bureau of Business and Economic Research, University of Nevada, Reno.

Lesieur, Henry R. 1997. "Measuring the Costs of Pathological Gambling." Paper presented at the Eleventh Annual Conference on Problem Gambling, New Orleans, August.

Lesieur, Henry R. 1998a. Testimony for the Expert Panel on Pathological Gambling, National Gambling Impact Study Commission, Atlantic City, NJ, January 22.

Lesieur, Henry R. 1998b. "Costs and Treatment of Pathological Gambling." *The Annals,* 556 (March): 153–169.

Lesieur, Henry R., and Christopher W. Anderson. 1995. *Results of a Survey of Gamblers Anonymous Members in Illinois.* Park Ridge, IL: Illinois Council on Problem and Compulsive Gambling.

Lesieur, Henry R., and Sheila B. Blume. 1987. "The South Oaks Gambling Screen (SOGS): A New Instrument for the Identification of Pathological Gamblers." *American Journal of Psychiatry,* 144: 1184–1188.

Lesieur, Henry R., and Sheila B. Blume. 1993. "Revising the South Oaks Gambling Screen in Different Settings." *Journal of Gambling Studies,* 9 (Fall): 213–219.

Lesieur, Henry R., and M. Heineman. 1988. "Pathological Gambling among Youthful Multiple Substance Abusers in a Therapeutic Community." *British Journal of Addiction,* 83: 765–771.

Lesieur, Henry R., and Robert Klein. 1985. *"Prisoners, Gambling, and Crime."* Paper presented at the Academy of Criminal Justice Sciences Annual Meeting, Las Vegas, NV.

Lesieur, Henry R., and R. Rosenthal. 1991. "Pathological Gambling: A Review of the Literature." *Journal of Gambling Studies,* 7: 5-40.

Lesieur, Henry R., and J. Rothschild. 1989. "Children of Gamblers Anonymous Members." *Journal of Gambling Behavior,* 5 (Winter): 269-282.

Lesieur, Henry R., et al. 1991. "Gambling and Pathological Gambling among University Students." *Addictive Behaviors,* 16: 517-527.

Lindner, R. M. 1950. "The Psychodynamics of Gambling." *The Annals,* 269 (May): 93–107.

Lorenz, Valerie. 1981. "Differences Found among Catholic, Protestant, and Jewish Families of Pathological Gamblers." Paper presented at the Fifth National Conference on Gambling and Risk Taking.

Lorenz, Valerie, and D.E. Shuttlesworth. 1983. "The Impact of Pathological Gambling on the Spouse of the Gambler." *Journal of Community Psychology,* 11: 67–74.

McAneny, Leslie. 1992. "Gambling Behavior." *The Gallup Poll Monthly,* December, pp. 5-11.

McGlothlin, W.H. 1954. "A Psychometric Study of Gambling." *Journal of Consulting Psychology,* 18: 145-149.

Merton, Robert K. 1957. *Social Theory and Social Structure.* New York: Free Press.

Meyer, G., et al. 1995. "The Social Costs of Pathological Gambling." Paper presented at the First European Conference on Gambling Studies and Policy Issues, St. John's College, Cambridge, United Kingdom, August.

Miller, D.C., and J.P. Byrnes. 1997. "The Role of Contextual and Personal Factors in Children's Risk Taking." *Developmental Psychology,* 33, no. 5: 814-823.

Morris, R.P. 1957. "An Exploratory Study of Some Personality Characteristics of Gamblers." *Journal of Clinical Psychology,* 13: 191–193.

National Council on Problem Gambling. N.d. "Overview of Compulsive Gambling." New York: National Council on Problem Gambling.

Niederland, W. 1967. "A Contribution to the Psychology of Gambling." *Psychoanalytic Forum,* 2: 175-185.

Phillips, David P., et al. 1997. "Elevated Suicide Levels Associated with Legalized Gambling." *Suicide and Life-Threatening Behavior,* 27 (Winter): 373-378.

Rosecrance, John. 1985. "Compulsive Gambling and the Medicalization of Deviance." *Social Problems,* 32 (February): 275-284.

Rosenthal, Richard J., and Henry R. Lesieur. 1992. "Self-Reported Withdrawal Symptoms and Pathological Gambling." *American Journal of Addictions,* 1: 150-154.

Roston, Ronald A. 1961. "Some Personality Characteristics of Male Compulsive Gamblers." Ph. D. diss., University of California—Los Angeles.

Schaffer, Howard J., and Matthew N. Hall. 1996. "Estimating the Prevalence of Adolescent Gambling Disorders: A Quantitative Synthesis and Guide Toward Standard Gambling Nomenclature." *Journal of Gambling Studies,* 12 (Summer): 193-214.

Schaffer, Howard J., et al. 1997. "Estimating the Prevalence of Disordered Gambling Behavior in the United States and Canada: A Meta-Analysis." Cambridge, MA: Harvard Medical School.

Smart, R.G., and J. Ferris. 1996. "Alcohol, Drugs, and Gambling in the Ontario Adult Population." *Canadian Journal of Psychiatry,* 41: 36-45.

Taber, Julian I., et al. 1986. "Ego Strength and Achievement Motivation in Pathological Gamblers." *Journal of Gambling Behavior,* 2 (Fall/Winter): 69-80.

Thompson, William N., et al. 1996. *The Social Costs of Gambling in Wisconsin.* Thiensville, WI: Wisconsin Policy Research Institute.

U.S. Bureau of the Census. 1996. *Statistical Abstract of the United States: 1996.* 116th ed. Washington, DC: U.S. Government Printing Office.

Volberg, Rachel. 1993. *Gambling and Problem Gambling among Native Americans in North Dakota.* Albany, NY: Gemini Research.

Volberg, Rachel. 1995. *Gambling and Problem Gambling in Iowa: A Replication Survey.* Report to the Iowa Department of Human Services. Roaring Springs, PA: Gemini Research.

Volberg, Rachel. 1996. "Prevalence Studies of Problem Gambling in the United States." *Journal of Gambling Studies,* 12 (Summer): 111-128.

Walker, Michael B. 1989. "Some Problems with the Concept of 'Gambling Addiction': Should Theories of Addiction Be Generalized to Include Excessive Gambling?" *Journal of Gambling Behavior,* 5 (Fall): 179-200.

Wallisch, Lynn S. 1993. *Gambling in Texas: 1992 Texas Survey of Adult Gambling Behavior.* Austin: Texas Commission on Alcohol and Drug Abuse.

Wallisch, Lynn S. 1996. *Gambling in Texas: 1995 Surveys of Adult and Adolescent Gambling Behavior.* Austin: Texas Commission on Alcohol and Drug Abuse.

Winters, Ken C., et al. 1993a. "Toward the Development of an Adolescent Gambling Problem Severity Scale." *Journal of Gambling Studies,* 9 (Spring): 63-84.

Winters, Ken C., et al. 1993b. "Patterns and Characteristics of Adolescent Gambling." *Journal of Gambling Studies,* 9 (Winter): 371-386.

Chapter 10

American Gaming Association. 1997. News Release, January 28.

Blaszczynski, Alex, and Derrick Silove. 1995. "Cognitive and Behavioral Therapies for Pathological Gambling." *Journal of Gambling Studies,* 11 (Summer): 195-220.

Brown, R.I.F. 1986. "Dropouts and Continuers in Gamblers Anonymous: Life

Context and Other Factors." *Journal of Gambling Behavior,* 2 (Fall/Winter): 130-140.

Brown, R.I.F. 1987a. "Dropouts and Continuers in Gamblers Anonymous. Part 2: Analysis of Free-Style Accounts of Experiences with GA." *Journal of Gambling Behavior,* 3 (Spring): 68-79.

Brown, R.I.F. 1987b. "Dropouts and Continuers in Gamblers Anonymous. Part 3: Some Possible Specific Reasons for Dropout." *Journal of Gambling Behavior,* 3 (Summer): 137-151.

Browne, Basil R. 1991. "The Selective Adaptation of the Alcoholics Anonymous Program by Gamblers Anonymous." *Journal of Gambling Studies,* 7 (Fall): 187-206.

Browne, Basil R. 1994. "Not Really God: Secularization and Pragmatism in Gamblers Anonymous." *Journal of Gambling Studies,* 10 (Fall): 247-260.

Cox, Sue, et al. 1997. "Problem and Pathological Gambling in America: The National Picture." Columbia, MD: National Council on Problem Gambling.

Custer, Robert, and Harry Milt. 1985. *When Luck Runs Out: Help for Compulsive Gamblers and Their Families.* New York: Facts on File Publications.

Deland, P.S. 1950. "The Facilitation of Gambling." *The Annals,* 269: 21-29.

Dickerson, Mark. 1984. *Compulsive Gamblers.* London: Longman.

Dickerson, Mark, et al. 1979. "Controlled Gambling as a Therapeutic Technique for Compulsive Gamblers." *Journal of Behavior Therapy and Experimental Psychiatry,* 10: 139-141.

Fingarette, Herbert. 1988. *Heavy Drinking: The Myth of Alcoholism as a Disease.* Berkeley: University of California Press.

Franklin, Joanna, and Donald R. Thoms. 1989. "Clinical Observations of Family Members of Compulsive Gamblers." In Howard J. Schaffer et al., *Compulsive Gambling: Theory, Research, and Practice,* pp. 135-146. Lexington, MA: Lexington Books.

Gwynne, S.C. 1997. "How Casinos Hook You." *Time,* November 27, pp. 68-69.

Hayano, David M. 1982. *Poker Faces.* Berkeley: University of California Press.

Horovitz, Bruce. 1997. "Harrah's Rolls Out Visa Card with Reward Plan." *USA Today,* October 23.

Lesieur, Henry R. 1990. "Working with and Understanding Gamblers Anonymous." In T.J. Powell, ed., *Working with Self Help,* pp. 237-253. Silver Spring, MD: NASW Press.

Lesieur, Henry R. 1998. "Costs and Treatment of Pathological Gambling." *The Annals,* 556 (March): 153–169.

Lesieur, Henry R., and Robert L. Custer. 1984. "Pathological Gambling: Roots, Phases, and Treatment." *The Annals,* 474 (July): 146-156.

Livingston, Jay. 1974. *Compulsive Gamblers: Observations on Action and Abstinence.* New York: Harper and Row.

Lorenz, Valerie C., and Robert A. Yaffee. 1989. "Pathological Gamblers and Their Spouses: Problems in Interaction." *Journal of Gambling Behavior,* 5 (Summer): 113-126.

National Council on Problem Gambling. 1993. *The Need for a National Policy on Problem and Pathological Gambling in America.* New York: National Council on Problem Gambling.

Oldman, David. 1978. "Compulsive Gamblers." *Sociological Review,* 26 (May): 349-370.

Palermo, Dave. 1998. "Admitting There's a Problem." *Gaming and Wagering Business,* 19, no. 1: 40.

Preston, Frederick W., and Ronald W. Smith. 1975. "Types and Treatments of Compulsive Gambling: Transferring the AA Paradigm." Paper presented at the Second Annual Conference on Gambling, Lake Tahoe, NV, June.

Preston, Frederick W., and Ronald W. Smith. 1985. "Delabeling and Relabeling in Gamblers Anonymous: Problems with Transferring the Alcoholics Anonymous Paradigm." *Journal of Gambling Behavior,* 1 (Fall/Winter): 97-105.

Rankin, Howard. 1982. "Control Rather Than Abstinence as a Goal in the Treatment of Excessive Gambling." *Behavior Research and Therapy,* 20: 185-187.

Rosecrance, John. 1988. *Gambling Without Guilt.* Pacific Grove, CA: Brooks/Cole.

Rosenthal, Richard J., and Loreen J. Rugle. 1994. "A Psychodynamic Approach to the Treatment of Pathological Gambling. Part I; Achieving Abstinence." *Journal of Gambling Studies,* 10 (Spring): 21-42.

Scott, Marvin. 1968. *The Racing Game.* Chicago: Aldine.

Stewart, Ruth M., and R.I. Brown. "An Outcome Study of Gamblers Anonymous." *British Journal of Psychiatry,* 152: 284-288.

Taber, Julian I. 1985. "Pathological Gambling: The Initial Screening Interview." *Journal of Gambling Behavior,* 1 (Spring/Summer): 23-34.

Zion, Maxene M., et al. 1991. "Examining the Relationship Between Spousal Involvement in Gam-Anon and Relapse Behaviors in Pathological Gamblers." *Journal of Gambling Studies,* 7 (Summer): 117-131.

Chapter 11

Connor, Matt. 1997. "Rules of the Game Need Definition." *Gaming and Wagering Business,* 18, no. 4 (April): 53.

Haring, Bruce. 1998. "Gambling: A High-Stakes Internet Game." *USA Today,* January 21, p. 4D.

Kenosha News. 1998. "Federal Judge: State Can Sue Company, Not Tribe, for Internet Lotto." *Kenosha News,* February 20, p. A7.

McKeag, Jana. 1997. "Feds Ponder Internet Regulation." *Gaming and Wagering Business,* 18, no. 6 (June): 78.

McQueen, Patricia A. 1997. "Bordering on Growth." *Gaming and Wagering Business,* 18, no. 4 (April): 55.

New View. 1998. "Navajos Turn Down Casino Proposal." *New View: Newsletter of the Texas Commission on Alcohol and Drug Abuse,* 8, no. 1 (January): 5.

Parets, Robyn Taylor. 1996. "Fasten Your Seatbelts." *Gaming and Wagering Business,* 17, no. 10 (October): 133-134.

Rose, I. Nelson. 1997. "Nevada OKs 'Net Gaming.'" *Casino Executive Magazine,* 3 (October): 32.

Schoenstein, Ralph. 1997. "Making Friendly Wagers in the Skies." *New York Times,* July 6, Sec. XX, p. 17.

Sinclair, Sebastian. 1997. "Sports Betting Heads to the Web." *Gaming and Wagering Business,* 18, no. 6 (June): 16.

Author Index

183

Subject Index